Miscarriage and Stillbirth

the changing response

A resource for families,
those in pastoral ministry
and healthcare providers

BRUCE PIERCE

Association For The
Promotion Of
Christian Knowledge

VERITAS

For Carol and Luke and in memory of my parents

First published 2003 by
Veritas Publications
7/8 Lower Abbey Street
Dublin 1
Ireland
Email publications@veritas.ie
Website www.veritas.ie

ISBN 1 85390 810 x

10 9 8 7 6 5 4 3 2 1

A catalogue record for this book is available from the British Library.

Cover design by Declan Kenny
Printed in the Republic of Ireland by The Leinster Leader, Naas, Co Kildare

*Veritas books are printed on paper made from the wood pulp of managed forests. For
every tree felled, at least one tree is planted, thereby renewing natural resources.*

Contents

Foreword by Prof. Tom O'Dowd   5

Preface   7

1   Miscarriage and Stillbirth – The Reality Today   11

2   The Past Responses of Society and the Church   18

3   Grief and the Nature of Loss   24

4   Loss Following Miscarriage and Stillbirth   30

5   The Caring Professions   55

6   What Really Helps the Bereaved   64

7   Rituals – Funerals, Prayers and Practice   72

8   Can Our Baby be Baptised?   81

9   Those Who Share the Journey – Support Groups   91

10   Future Developments   99

11   Liturgies following Miscarriage or Stillbirth   102
        Blessing of a child   102
        Blessing of a stillborn baby   103
        A service for all faiths   104
        A service for the family in a home setting   106
        Funeral service for a baby   109
        Memorial service to remember precious babies   112

12   Occasional Prayers, Meditations, Poems and Other
        Resources   116

13   Principles of Good Practice for Professionals   133

        Web Resources   138
        Selected Bibliography   140
        Index   142

Foreword

'When death and birth collide at the same time', as happens in miscarriage and stillbirth, many people do not know what to say or do. They will feel confused and sad that the natural order of parents dying before their child is turned upside down and they will be terrified of saying the wrong thing.

Not knowing what to say is common among other parents, doctors and clergy. There has been a trend of improvement in our perspectives on miscarriage and stillbirth but there is still a long way to go. Thanks to bereaved parents and research we now have guidelines to cope with our own helplessness and our need to express our sadness to the bereaved.

There has long been a need for a reference source that turns the evidence of bereaved parents and researchers into practical advice. This book will be invaluable for the bereaved, for doctors, clergy, social workers, self-help groups and for those who want simply to express their sadness to the bereaved parents. Bruce Pierce's book is a restrained mixture of evidence, compassion and learning. Uniquely, it can be used at a practical level and also for reflection on the cruelty of loss amid hope and expectation.

Tom O'Dowd
Professor of General Practice
Trinity College, Dublin

Preface

When your parent dies, you have lost your past.
When your child dies, you have lost your future.[1]

One spring morning I walked briskly through the Holy Angels'
Plot in Glasnevin Cemetery, Dublin. In my hand I had a copy of
the Register of Interments for those buried in this open space.
I focused on the reference for a grave location – PA 122 South.
Marching out the required number of paces on this open space
decorated with flowers, grave markers and headstones made by
parents, I arrived under a small tree near the wall. Here in an
unmarked grave lay my older brother, Rodney, who had died of
'delicacy' some forty-four years previously. He had lived for two
days and was buried on Christmas Eve.

No one attended his funeral. My father, who described his
full head of black hair, saw him briefly. Rodney was never seen
by my mother – 'it was for the best' she had been told. Over the
years little pieces of his story came together. The advice was
given to have another child as soon as possible and to get on
with things. Kindnesses shown by family and friends were treasured, as also may have been those unhelpful words and actions.

Spoken of often was the gentle pastoral presence of the Rector who visited and baptised Rodney a few hours after he was born.

From that spring morning journey I finalised my decision on the subject matter for an impending thesis: 'Ritual Denied – Ritual Granted; Changing Pastoral Perspectives on Miscarriage and Stillbirth'. This book is a continuation of that theme.

I hope this work will be of assistance to those in ministry whose role is so crucial in both the early days and in the months and years that follow the death of a baby. It may also be of assistance and provide insights to colleagues in other healthcare professions. My wish is that bereaved parents, on reading it, will realise that all those strange feelings and emotions they have experienced are 'normal' and are part of the grief journey after this most painful of losses. Another desire for this book is that it will acknowledge the professional and appropriate care that is now being given to bereaved parents. Finally, I would hope that in this book the work of the support groups is acknowledged and celebrated for what it is.

In writing this book I have many people to thank. Firstly, I am most grateful to those parents who were prepared to tell their stories in order that 'it might help others'. I gratefully acknowledge the generosity of my colleagues in ministry who freely shared their work, thoughts and resources. To the following chaplain colleagues I express my thanks: Fr Kevin Doherty, Sr Eliza Hopkins, Rev. Fred Appelbe, Rev. David Skuce, Rev. Blair Robertson, Canon Michael Burgess, Very Rev. John Patterson, Betty Lynch Power, Rev. Fred Coutts, Rev. James Falconer, Kathleen Graham and many others too numerous to list. Acknowledgements are given where possible in the text.

I would like to thank Kevin Egan, my thesis supervisor from All Hallows College, Dublin, and other members of staff who suggested that the thesis could go a little further. Throughout the work for this book I have received immeasurable support from Ron Smith Murphy (Chairperson of ISANDS – Irish Stillbirth and Neonatal Death Society). I would also wish to thank the members of the committee of ISANDS. A second support group I wish to thank is MAI (Miscarriage Association of Ireland), and in particular Maggie O'Neill. I am very grateful to Prof. Tom O'Dowd for kindly agreeing to write the foreword to the book and also to Dr Kevin Connolly and Sheila Beckett for their assistance. Thanks, too, to David and Karen Seaman for their patience and persistence as proof readers.

A number of institutions have been very generous in supporting my studies in this area. I acknowledge, with gratitude, the support of (former Archbishop) Walton Empey and the United Dioceses of Dublin and Glendalough, the Adelaide Hospital Society and the Adelaide & Meath Hospital (Incorporating the National Children's Hospital) at Tallaght, Dublin. I am appreciative of the generous financial support given by the National Children's Hospital Foundation to fund the publishing of this book. I am also appreciative of the assistance of Catherine McDaid, CEO of AMNCH Hospital.

My sincere thanks to Diane Midland and Fran Rybarik of RTS Bereavement Training Programme at Gundersen Lutheran Medical Foundation. For those wishing to pursue further training in the area of perinatal death I can thoroughly recommend the work of RTS.

I would especially like to extend my thanks to Canon Kenneth Kearon, Director of the Irish School of Ecumenics, for his ongoing assistance and wisdom. As this book was finalised while out of Ireland, I am deeply indebted to Rev. Bernie Daly for her constant support and ongoing assistance. I would also like to thank both APCK and Veritas for their commitment.

Finally, this book would have remained as a bundle of papers on my study floor, were it not for the enthusiastic encouragement of my wife, Carol.

Notes

1.   Luby, E., 'Bereavement and grieving' in Schiff, H., *The Bereaved Parent* (Penguin Books, New York, 1977), p.23.

Dear Parents

I did not die young.
I lived my span of life
Within your body
And within your love.
There are many
Who have lived long lives
And have not been loved as me.
If you would honour me
Then speak my name
And number me among your family.
If you would honour me
Then strive to live in love
For, in that love, I live.
Never ever doubt
That we will meet again.
Until that happy happy day
I will grow with God
And wait for you.

© Christy Kenneally, from *Life After Loss* (Mercier Press, Cork)

1
Miscarriage and Stillbirth – The Reality Today

On hearing the news that a baby has just been born, the question often expressed is: 'And is everything all right?' For parents who journey through pregnancy, the greatest fear often centres upon what the outcome will be at delivery. Parents celebrate with great joy when their baby is born. Simultaneously, there is profound relief as they cradle their living child.

What happens when the baby dies, when, in the words of Lovell, 'death and birth collide at the same time'? There is no celebration. Instead, all the hopes and wishes of the parents are shattered; the months of anticipation, planning and excitement are extinguished in those few words that are used to tell them their baby is dead. Equally, but often not acknowledged, is the similar emotional turmoil that ensues when a mother has a miscarriage.

This book tells part of the story of how things once were for parents whose babies died during pregnancy or at birth. In the past, neither society in general nor the Church acknowledged such grief or responded to it. This was a time when both recognition of loss and the need for ritual were denied. Such a bereavement was not seen as a real loss because there was no person to grieve for. This lack of acknowledgement of the depth of loss had, of course, implications for what was seen as appropriate aftercare. Phrases were used to help, such as 'It wasn't as if it was a real child' or 'You never knew it, so that will make it easier'. Such expressions of sympathy did little to help; often they led to a situation where parents believed they should not even speak about what had happened. These real losses were denied and those who wished to talk about them felt isolated and unheard.

Changes occurred slowly in the response of society and, some would suggest, even more slowly in the pastoral response of the Church. This journey of change came about through the actions of individuals and members of support groups who were courageous enough to say that this loss was real. It was when these voices were eventually listened to, that the various responses began to change. It was only then that the need for ritual began to be recognised.

Changes in attitudes have led to changes in practice. Within the following pages current practice will be examined from the perspective of bereaved parents, clergy and members of the healthcare professions. The vital role of the various support groups will be discussed. Many parents believe that without the support groups these crucial changes would not have occurred.

Current practice is not the final part of the story. As this book will acknowledge, issues still remain for parents and these need to be addressed honestly and clearly. The concerns of bereaved parents on the quality and relevance of the liturgy being offered continue to be expressed. For some parents, the refusal of the sacrament of baptism continues to hurt and marginalise. Parents who suffer a miscarriage often have a feeling that their own loss is not acknowledged, especially if it happens early in the pregnancy.

Crucial to the care of bereaved parents is the involvement of the various healthcare professionals, clergy, family and friends. The quality and appropriateness of care is vital for parents in the face of their loss. These various caring roles will be acknowledged in this book, as they are by so many parents.

Definitions

It is important to be clear about the definitions that we use in this area. In comparing different definitions there must be an awareness of the cultural and legal understandings that exist in different situations. In addition, it must be acknowledged that legal definitions do not take into account or have any real connection with the emotions present in parents following the death of their baby. However, these definitions can greatly influence the response of the caring professions to the parents.

Miscarriage

Miscarriage refers to a baby who is born dead before the legal age of viability: twenty-four weeks. (October 1992, UK[1]; January 1995, Ireland.) Babies who die in this category have, as yet, no legal standing. Miscarriage can be divided initially into either of two experiences:

- Incomplete miscarriage is a pregnancy loss in which not all the products of conception are passed from the womb. Following such a loss the mother would require a surgical procedure (Dilation and Curettage).
- Complete miscarriage is a pregnancy loss in which all the products of conception are passed from the womb. Such losses tend to be before 6-8 weeks or after 14-16 weeks.

Types of miscarriage
1. Ectopic pregnancy occurs when a fertilised egg has difficulty moving down the fallopian tube and becomes implanted in an ovary, cervix or abdomen. This can happen very early in pregnancy and the woman may not be aware of it. One of the unique aspects of such a loss is that it may not be cared for as a standard pregnancy loss. Due to the suddenness of the need for a medical response, the emphasis may be placed solely upon the life of the mother.

2. Blighted ovum is a pregnancy in which the gestational sac is seen but within which the embryo does not develop.

3. Molar pregnancy is a pregnancy in which a placental tumour develops and subsequently the embryo dies while the placenta continues to grow.

Stillbirth

A stillbirth was defined in Section 41 of the Births and Deaths Registration Act 1953 (UK) as 'a child which has issued forth from its mother after the twenty-eighth week of pregnancy, and which did not at any time after becoming completely expelled from its mother breathe or show other signs of life'. From 1 October 1992, within the United Kingdom, the legal definition of a stillbirth was altered from a baby born dead after twenty-eight completed weeks' gestation or more, to one born dead after twenty-four completed weeks' gestation or more. This change arose from medical advances, which put the likelihood of viability forward from twenty-eight weeks to twenty-four weeks.[2]

In 1994 the Irish Government introduced the Stillbirths Registration Act, which applies in relation to a child born weighing 500 grams or more, or having a gestational age of twenty-four weeks or more, who shows no sign of life at birth.[3] The important role of the support group ISANDS was crucial in bringing about this change. Within parts of the USA, stillbirth is defined as a death after twenty weeks' gestation, when the baby weighs 350 grams or more. A changing definition has, of course, implications for how the loss is viewed.

Within the terms of this Irish Act there is now open-ended retrospective registration for bereaved parents of a stillborn baby. After a stillbirth, the law requires certain procedures, which in themselves imply certain moral obligations, which come from the recognition of the status of the stillborn baby.

However, for parents whose babies die prior to the twenty-four weeks point, there are no legal requirements, no official statistics and no standard practice. This dividing line of twenty-four weeks can make a major significance to the experience and grief journey of bereaved parents.

It has been noted that it is the personal significance of the loss, and not the gestational age of the baby, that determines the extent of the parents' bereavement and their need to grieve.[4] Research will be quoted at a later stage, which sets out that the loss experienced by a mother from an early miscarriage can be both very profound and traumatic.[5]

Though not within the scope of this book, reference needs to be made to neonatal death. While there are many similarities with the loss of a baby that has lived for even a few moments, there are also differences. A baby who dies after birth is entitled to both a birth and a death certificate. Such tangible confirmation does express clearly that a baby did actually live, even for a few minutes. This can be very important for bereaved parents. In addition, the possibility of baptism, and also the existence of photographs of a live baby, can be very helpful to parents.

Statistics

Miscarriage, the spontaneous loss of a pregnancy within the first twenty-four weeks, occurs in approximately a fifth of all known pregnancies.[6] It is estimated that up to 75 per cent of all human conceptions do not result in the birth of a live born baby but are lost at some point in the pregnancy.[7] In many cases mothers are neither aware of the conception nor of the loss. These figures for miscarriage are based, of course, upon informed guesses. The Miscarriage Association (UK) estimates that approximately 160,000 to 200,000 confirmed pregnancies end annually in miscarriage within the UK.[8]

Miscarriage is overwhelmingly the most frequent among all types of pregnancy loss. Past reproductive history is the most relevant predictive factor in a subsequent pregnancy.[9] Recurrent miscarriage, the loss of three or more consecutive pregnancies, can be very traumatic for parents and affects 1 per cent of all women.[10] Research has shown that male infants have an excessive risk of neonatal death in comparison to females. The reason for this remains unclear.

Statistically, the number of stillbirths is much lower and can be assessed accurately. According to the Royal College of Obstetrics and Gynaecology, in 1997 in England and Wales there were 3440 stillbirths, which leads to a rate of 5.1/1000. Statistics for 1996, again for England and Wales, show that 0.5 per cent of pregnancies end in stillbirth after twenty-four weeks' gestation.[11] In Scotland there were 351 stillbirths and a rate of 6.1 per 1000 total births during 1998. In Ireland there were 297 stillbirths with a rate of 6.1 during 1994.[12] Looking at the statistics for one of the major Dublin hospitals in 1999, the following figures apply:[13]

Mothers delivered of infant weighing 500 grams +	6970.0
Spontaneous miscarriages	676.0
Ectopic pregnancies	23.0
Total number of mothers	7669.0
Total stillbirths	38.0
Stillbirth rate (per 1000 births)	5.4

Notes:

1. Smith, N., *Miscarriage, Stillbirth and Neonatal Death*, Joint Committee for Hospital Chaplaincy (Ludo Press, London, 1993), p.3.

2. Lovell, Alice, *A Bereavement with a Difference* (South Bank University, London, 1995), p.7.

3. General Register Office, S.B. Info Leaflet No. 1, *How Parents can Register their Stillborn Child (born before 1 January, 1995).*

4. Kohner, N., & Henley, A., *When a Baby Dies* (HarperCollins, London, 1991).

5. Allen, M. & Marks, S., *Miscarriage: Women Sharing from the Heart* (John Wiley & Sons, New York, 1993).

6. Slade, P., and Cecil, R., 'Understanding the experience and emotional consequences of miscarriage' in *Journal of Reproductive and Infant Psychology*, Vol. 12, 1994, p.1.

7. Oakley, A., McPherson, A. and Roberts, H., *Miscarriage* (1984), quoted in Lovell, op. cit., 1995, p.7.

8. Smith, N., *Miscarriage, Stillbirth and Neonatal Death*, Joint Committee for Hospital Chaplaincy (Ludo Press, London, 1993), p.1.

9. Regan, L., Braude, P.R., and Trembath, P.L., 'Influences of past reproductive performance on risk of spontaneous abortion' in *British Medical Journal* 299, 1989, p.541.

10. Stirrat, G.M., 'Recurrent miscarriage: definition and epidemiology' in *Lancet* 336, 1990, pp.673-5.

11. Office of National Statistics (Series FM1), No. 25, 1998.

12. Central Statistics Office, *Report on Vital Statistics* (Stationery Office, Dublin, 1998), p.38.

13. Annual Clinical Report of Coombe Women's Hospital (Dublin, 1999).

2

The Past Responses of Society and the Church

In the earliest historical writings on miscarriage and stillbirth, the loss was seen solely in terms of the loss of a possession by the father. Exodus 21:22–25 states that if a woman miscarries following a blow from a man, her husband is entitled to set the level of a fine, subject to the court's approval. The Assyrian Laws were similar, punishing the assault severely as an invasion of the husband's property. In almost all cases, women were understood in relationship to a male and not as individuals in their own right. The lack of material on this subject in Scripture or other religious writings may mean that on occasion the religious and cultural needs of parents may not be met.

From the world of literature there are a number of references that set out the views of the past. Shakespeare, in *Henry V*, articulates a sense of guilt associated with the death of a foetus:

> *For her male issue*
> *Either died where they were made,*
> *Or shortly after this world had aired them;*
> *Hence I took a thought,*
> *This was a judgement on me.*

In nineteenth-century literature, references to miscarriage and stillbirth are not uncommon but are given minimum attention. In Thomas Hardy's *The Mayor of Casterbridge*, the impact of the miscarriage of Lucetta is presented as being of little significance in itself. The main tragedy lies in the consequent death of the would-be mother. In George Eliot's *Middlemarch*, the miscarriage of Rosamund is mentioned in a similar manner. The evidence suggests that pregnancy loss was not considered a subject worthy of significant literary attentions. At a much later stage Margaret Mitchell, in *Gone with the Wind* (1936), included considerable discussion of miscarriage, incorporating within it a study of its emotional and physical effects on Scarlett O'Hara.

How things were

As part of the background to this book the experiences of those bereaved in a timeframe greater than twenty years and those bereaved in the last five years were compared and contrasted. Those bereaved a long time ago, described a society where paternalistic attitudes permeated the healthcare system. Parents were encouraged to allow the hospital to look after things. Parents often did not hold or even see their baby. The practice was for the baby to be removed as quickly as possible and access to it was discouraged. Parents were not encouraged to attend the funeral, if there was one. Neither funeral notices nor acknowledgements in the daily papers would have been considered. Instead, it was suggested to parents that they should have another child as soon as possible.

Dotted around the Irish countryside there are burial grounds called *cillíní*, often situated near the walls of consecrated ground. Here, the unbaptised were buried. Accounts exist of family members climbing over the wall at night to bury an infant in consecrated ground. The issue of limbo, the place perceived as the resting-place for the souls of unbaptised infants, is still a real issue to some parents. This will be explored at a later stage.

Rosanne Cecil undertook a study in Northern Ireland covering the period from the 1940s, 1950s and the beginning of the 1960s, apropos elderly women's recollections of their pregnancy losses.[1] She made interesting observations on how these losses were treated by society and by the women themselves. The dominating feature was a prevailing and veiled culture of silence. From her research she noted that those women who had been bereaved up to fifty years previously, had not told their story very often. Discussion was limited within the family circle and little, if anything, went beyond that circle. Women were very excluded from what followed the death of their baby. If there had been a ritual, women certainly would not have attended.

Cecil refers to a society where, until the 1960s, unbaptised children were not usually buried in consecrated ground because the 'Church did not regard them as part of its community'.[2] Whatever liturgy took place, if any, was minimal, with miscarriage burials being at night so that no one would witness them. Further, she demonstrated that in Belfast there existed a direct correlation between the burial place of a dead baby and its perceived status and value within society: 'in their unmarked graves is symbolised their social worth'. Stillborn babies were viewed as not really full members of society and, therefore, were put in different burial grounds.

Brady et al. (1984),[3] in their extensive research of 1980, also commented on the burial of the stillborn babies in a communal grave. They compared the open piece of ground used for infants with the nearby well-ordered and clearly defined adult graves. Cecil sums up her research by stating that for these now elderly women reflecting on the past, there was a real significance to their loss. There was real regret expressed at the lack of any formal ritual to say goodbye. There was also regret by the women at the perceived non-value of their baby by society.

Over the last twenty-five years, changing social, cultural and ecclesiastical attitudes have led to changes in the pastoral response to bereaved parents. It is only when the needs of a group have been acknowledged as having value by society at large, that change will follow to meet these needs. The informed consensus posits that the specific needs of bereaved parents have only in the present day been acknowledged by society and by the Church – a process that has taken over a quarter of a century. In the process of acknowledgement, change has occurred and become manifest in the pastoral response of society, not least through the work of those in the healthcare professions and the Churches. However, it is a journey that still has further to go.

The journey to changes in attitudes and practice

The nature of current practice will be explored later in the book. For now, suffice to say that, in general, the response is more inclusive of the parents' wishes and needs. However, there are still occasions when the care offered is neither appropriate nor helpful. The change in attitude, at times quite radical, was connected to the contribution of the various support groups who lobbied and became the voice for those who could not speak of their grief. Also to be acknowledged is a small but vocal group of professionals who at times, in conjunction with the support groups, articulated the needs of parents.

The first research undertaken in the United Kingdom in this area was by two nurses, Bruce[4] and McLenahan,[5] in 1962. As a sign of the times, no hospital allowed Bruce to conduct such a research programme, as it would be too upsetting for mothers. In Sweden during 1963 Johan Cullberg, a psychiatrist, undertook the first systematic study and noted the importance of mothers being allowed to express their emotions following the death of their baby. He also noted how some in the medical profession preferred to reduce the emotional outbursts to a more 'acceptable level'.

During 1970 Giles,[6] an Australian obstetrician, wrote on the importance of naming the baby and also on the need for funeral rites to confirm the reality of the loss. Kennell et al.,[7] writing in Ohio, highlighted the growing awareness of reality confrontation – the need and desire to see and hold the baby following the loss. They also noted the importance of this experience in parents' grief journey. Stanford Bourne and Emmanuel Lewis,[8] two London-based psychiatrists, together with two paediatricians, Hugh Jolly and David Morris, had pivotal roles in changing attitudes from the 1960s on. Bourne remarked on his difficulty in getting work published in the medical journals in the late 1960s; the reason given was that 'enough had already been published on the subject'.

In tandem with those from the medical profession, the media of the 1970s started to highlight this area of loss. In 1975 Hugh Jolly was involved in a battle with the Department of Health and Social Services (UK) who had sent a letter to hospitals asking them to arrange funerals of stillborn babies on parents' behalf. The idea was to 'save parents the additional stress of arranging a funeral for a child who had never lived'. He challenged this concept of the stillborn baby never living and also helped initiate change in burial law so that a funeral service could take place for a baby of less than twenty-eight weeks' gestation.

Alice Lovell,[9] a London-based sociologist, writing in 1983, moved the parameters of the discussion to include late miscarriage losses. She noted the so-called 'hierarchy of sadness' whereby miscarriage was seen as the smaller loss and a stillbirth as minor loss compared with the death of a newborn child. Her research showed findings that challenged this view.

With the growth of the support groups such as SANDS (Stillbirth and Neonatal Death Society) (UK), change in practice and public understanding of the nature of loss has also taken place. The important role of the various support groups will be explored later.

Collectively, those connected with the life of the Church have been slow in producing and responding to the challenges raised by such losses. It is interesting to compare the response to the needs of bereaved parents with the traditional championing of the life of the unborn child voiced by the Church. There seems to have been a silence on the part of the Church when it came to challenging both their own and society's practices, which downgraded the loss experienced by bereaved parents.

Notes:

1. Cecil, R., *The Anthropology of Pregnancy Loss* (Berg, Oxford, 1996), p.179.

2. Ibid., p.181.

3. Brady et al., 'Stillbirth: The mother's view' in *Irish Medical Journal*, Vol. 77, No. 5, 1984, p.137.

4. Bruce, S., 'Reactions of nurses and mothers to stillbirths' in *Nursing Outlook* 10 (2), 1962, pp.88-91.

5. McLenahan, I.G., 'Helping the mother who has no baby to bring home' in *American Journal of Nursing* 62 (4), 1962, pp.70-71.

6. Giles, P., 'Reaction of women to perinatal death' in *Australian and New Zealand Journal of Obstetrics and Gynaecology* 10, 1970, pp.207-10.

7. Kennell, J.H. and Klaus, M.H., 'Care of the mother of the high risk infant' in *Clinical Obstetrics and Gynaecology* 14, 1971, pp.926-54.

8. Bourne, S. and Lewis, E., 'Perinatal bereavement. A milestone and some new dangers' in *British Medical Journal* 302, 1991, pp.1167-8.

9. Lovell, A., 'Some questions of identity: late miscarriage, stillbirth and perinatal death' in *Social Science and Medicine* 17, 1983, pp.755-61.

3
Grief and the Nature of Loss

Grief is always related to loss. The word 'grief' comes from an Old English word, 'reafian'[1] which means 'to rob' – a sudden forceful deprivation. For many people this is their experience following the death of a loved one. The following brief definition may help where 'bereavement is the loss of a significant other person, which leads to a reaction called grief, which can be seen in a variety of behaviour patterns called mourning'.[2] Grief can refer to a wide range of experiences and so, for example, two individuals can be grieving and their experiences can differ considerably.

First and foremost it has to be acknowledged that grief cannot be compared, measured or quantified. Often society tries to compartmentalise grief and standardise how the bereaved should or should not react. Equally, society is perceived as allocating only a limited time to 'get over things'. Death has been widely acknowledged as something of a taboo subject and parts of society's practice seem committed to sanitising the process. While grief is natural, Gorer noted that mourning has been treated as if it were a weakness – 'a reprehensible bad habit instead of a psychological necessity'.[3]

Many writers hold the view that death is badly handled by modern society. Traditionally society used ritual, liturgy and religion to deal with death. With the increase of individualism and the decrease in the influence of religion, changes are inevitable. If such attitudes are still prevalent for adults who die, what then are the implications for pregnancy and newborn loss?

Grief theory in the twentieth century

Freud described the essence of mourning a loved person as 'painfully recalling memories of the deceased in detaching oneself from that relationship and of identifying, finally, with certain features of the loved one who had died'.[4] Some theorists advocated an approach to the goal of grief work as that of cutting the bond with the deceased. Clinebell (1984), for instance, articulates this viewpoint in writing: 'The grief wound cannot heal fully until one has accepted the reality of the loss, surrendered one's emotional tie to the lost person, and begun to form other relationships to provide new sources of interpersonal satisfaction'.[5]

The informed consensus among many theorists today points to the importance of establishing a new and changed bond with the person who has died as opposed to cutting bonds with the deceased. This allows the bereaved person to enter a new and enriching relationship. Klass (1996)[6] writes of how the bereaved interact with 'inner representations of the deceased' – a process quite different to wanting to separate and let go of the deceased. Interestingly, Klass undertook much of his research into the work of the support group Compassionate Friends, which helps bereaved parents. His research demonstrates and highlights the revised contemporary approach regarding grief resolution. Thus, rather than the emphasis being on the surrendering of 'one's emotional tie to the lost person' (see Clinebell, 1984, above), the emphasis is now upon altering the relationship with the deceased.

We can see a good example of this contemporary re-emphasising and theory development by comparing the first and second editions of William Worden's text, *Grief Counselling and Grief Therapy* (1991).

In the first edition Worden sets out the tasks of mourning as:

1. To accept the reality of the loss.
2. To experience the pain of grief.
3. To adjust to an environment in which the deceased is missing.
4. To withdraw emotional energy and reinvest in another relationship.

By the time of the second edition the author has amended the last task as 'to emotionally relocate the deceased and move on with life'.[7]

In the area of perinatal death, the work of John Bowlby and attachment theory is very relevant. Attachment theory sets out that individuals develop strong affectional bonds with other individuals. The breaking of these bonds, through death, is a traumatic experience and grief is an inbuilt and universal response to that separation. His initial work was based upon the relationship between a mother and her child. For both, there is an evolved biological need to stay in close contact with each other. Bowlby pointed out that the grieving of a bereaved adult was very similar to that of a young child whose mother had left. He went further and raised the idea that grief and mourning, following the death of a loved one, was a form of separation anxiety. When a separation occurs three responses can be identified: protest, despair and emotional detachment. The intensity of the grief is related to the extent of attachment.

Stages of grief

Many writers have suggested that there are stages through which a bereaved person must go. Among these are Lindemann (1944)[8] and Engel (1964)[9] who established an outline of the stages of mourning, which included protest, disorganisation and reorganisation. Further reflection on this understanding gave rise to particular theories regarding evolutionary stages in human development. Human behaviour was seen in terms of an evolving human potential towards an ultimate stage of stability or reintegration. Kubler-Ross[10] (1969) researched the views of the dying in terms of her five stages: denial and isolation, anger, bargaining, depression and finally acceptance. Many others followed this stage approach. One of the possible difficulties of a rigid application of this approach is that one needs to guard against inappropriate expectations of the bereaved.

Glen Davidson (1984)[11] set out four Phases of Bereavement, which allows for a more flexible grief journey than the rigid stage approach:

1. Shock and numbness: dominant in first two weeks.
2. Searching and yearning: dominant from second week to fourth month.
3. Disorientation: dominant from fifth to ninth month.
4. Reorganisation: dominant from eighteenth to twenty-fourth month.

Many present-day theorists no longer feel that grief resolution goes along such neat and anticipated stages. Some research suggests that the stage a bereaved person may be at, is more determined by personality make-up and environment than any inherent property of the stage in question.

Grief in a family setting

Death usually occurs within the family setting and this is especially the case with the majority of miscarriages and stillbirths. It is important to remember that every family is first and foremost a system. Up until the 1950s a family was seen in terms of a collection of individuals, but with the arrival of systems theory, led by family theorists such as Murray Bowen, a new approach to the family appeared. Every member of a family was now to be seen as part of many different relationships, whose attitudes, feelings, decisions and emotional growth are connected to others in the family system. In essence, with a family system approach, the behaviour of individuals is understood and measured in terms of how they function within the family, rather than as separate individuals.

In any system there is a tendency continually to strive, in self-corrective ways, to preserve the balance of the system – homeostasis. This balance must also struggle with the forces of togetherness and individuality, which are ongoing within each family member. This can be used to explain how families have major problems with change and, therefore, resist it.

Death is a trauma that greatly changes the balance of the relationships within the family. The death of a parent, spouse or child creates emptiness in the system, as well as in the lives of individual family members. Everything changes when there is a death. In caring for a bereaved family, an understanding of the systemic nature of family connections is very helpful.

In this chapter some of the evolving understanding of grief theory has been explored. Much of this information is very relevant for those caring for bereaved families following the death of a baby. In the following chapter the more specific grief experiences of bereaved parents and other family members will be addressed.

Notes:

1. Payne, S., Horn, S. & Relf. M., *Loss and Bereavement* (Open University, Buckingham, 1999), p.6.
2. Stroebe, M.S., Stroebe, W. and Hansson, R. (eds.), *Handbook of Bereavement* (Cambridge University Press, Cambridge, 1993), p.5.
3. Gorer, G., *Death, Grief and Mourning in Contemporary Britain* (Crescent Press, London, 1965), p.113.
4. Freud, S., 'Mourning and Melancholia' in *The Standard Edition of the Complete Psychological Works of Sigmund Freud*, ed. Strachey, J., Vol. 14, pp.239-58 (Hogarth Press, London, 1957).
5. Clinebell, H., *Basic Types of Pastoral Counselling: New Resources for the Troubled* (SCM Press, Washington, 1984), p.225.
6. Klass D., 'Spiritual Aspects of the Resolution of Grief' in *Dying: Facing the Facts*, eds. H. Wass and R. Neimeyer (Taylor & Francis, New York, 1996).
7. Worden, W., *Grief Counselling and Grief Therapy*, 2nd edn (Springer Publishing, New York, 1991), p.16.
8. Lindemann, E., 'Symptomatology and management of acute grief' in *American Journal of Psychiatry*, 101, 1944, pp.141-8.
9. Engel, G., 'Grief and Grieving' in *American Journal of Nursing*, 62, 1964, pp.93-8.
10. Kubler-Ross, E., *On Death and Dying* (Macmillan, New York, 1969).
11. Davidson, G., *Understanding Mourning* (Augsburg Publishing, Minneapolis House, 1984).

4
Loss Following Miscarriage and Stillbirth

Listen

When I ask you to listen to me and you start giving advice
you have not done what I've asked.
When I ask you to listen to me
and you begin to tell me why I shouldn't feel that way,
you are trampling on my feelings.
When I ask you to listen to me
and you feel you have something to solve my problems,
you have failed me, strange as that may seem.
Listen! All I asked was that you listen, not talk or do – just hear me.
Advice is cheap: 10 cents will get you both Dear Abby and
Billy Graham in the same newspaper.
And I can do for myself; I'm not helpless.
When you do something for me that I can and need to do
for myself, you contribute to my fear and weakness.
But, when you accept as a simple fact that I do feel what
I feel, no matter how irrational, then I can quit trying to
convince you and get about the business of understanding
what's behind this irrational feeling.
And when that's clear, the answers are obvious, and I don't need
advice.
Irrational feelings make sense when we understand what's behind
them. So, please listen and just hear me. And if you want to
talk, wait a minute for your turn; and I'll listen to you.

Anonymous[1]

The nature of pregnancy

Becoming pregnant is a major change that transforms a woman's life and expands her role to that of a mother. Much of the adaptation to this new role happens prior to delivery of her baby. For a mother, pregnancy is a period of radical change as the emphasis moves unto herself, her expected baby and her relationship with the father.

Central to the cycle of pregnancy is the concept of attachment. Kennell and Klaus (1996)[2] set out nine stages in this process of motherhood:

1. Planning the pregnancy
2. Confirming the pregnancy
3. Accepting the pregnancy
4. Feeling foetal movement
5. Accepting the foetus as an individual
6. Giving birth
7. Hearing and seeing the infant
8. Touching and holding the infant
9. Caring for the infant

The first five stages take place before the birth of the baby and this signifies the nature and strength of the attachment bond. Through pregnancy, a woman comes to 'know' her baby intimately and becomes attached both to the real and vibrant experience of her baby in the womb and also to her idealised image of who her child will be. During pregnancy parents visualise themselves in the role of parents. Such images are very much connected with their own parents' role. Being pregnant can give a real sense of personal contribution and value that transcends one's own life. It can lead to a sense of real worth, to status and self-esteem. It can also bring about a sense of healthy omnipotence.

The change in perception may occur quite early in a pregnancy. Researchers have noted that 30 per cent of married women who are *primagravida* (first-time mothers) think of the foetus as a real person between the eighth and the twelfth week of pregnancy. Connecting back to the work of Bowlby and attachment theory, one can see how the loss is very real given the strength of the attachment bond between a mother and her baby.

Misunderstandings about the nature of pregnancy loss

> *'Grief is part of a way of life that measles are not; to be wounded is not to be sick.'*[3]

One of the common misunderstandings of grief is that it is an illness, rather than a natural process following bereavement, especially in the case of miscarriage or stillbirth. The language we often use is about 'getting better soon'. When we speak of recovering, we speak as though the mother has had some unfortunate illness. The implication is that after a good rest all will be normal again. Equally, a father can be treated as someone whose partner is sick rather than as a father whose child has died.

Grief, however, should not be seen as something to be overcome, with the associated and implicit notion of cure. Society may in so many ways ignore or attempt to minimise the loss. Often these losses fail to be socially acknowledged or supported because it is not understood that the attachment bonds begin long before birth.

Miscarriage

The common causes of miscarriage are:

- Random, genetic error, e.g. chromosome abnormalities
- Low progesterone level or other hormonal factors
- Uterine structure not sufficient, e.g. weakened cervix
- Blighted ovum
- Infections, e.g. Rubella, Chlamydia
- Maternal diseases, e.g. Epilepsy, Diabetes
- Psychological factors – stress and anxiety
- Domestic violence

In comparison to other forms of pregnancy loss, miscarriage has certain unique aspects. Research shows clearly that for the majority of women who miscarry, their loss is seen as both a real loss and also as a loss of part of themselves. Allen & Marks (1993)[4] in a research project for mothers who experienced a pregnancy loss (in the range of 4-20 weeks) produced the following results:

- 30% of women had thoughts of suicide
- 38% had panic attacks
- 44% thought they were going crazy
- 48% doubted they would ever get through their grief
- 70% experienced their babies as whole and living human beings
- 1% of miscarriages were experienced as the death of their child
- 81% felt that a part of them had died

One of the implications from this research is that the experiences of such women must be listened to, in order that pastoral practices are appropriate to their needs. A key principle of pastoral practice is to base it upon the real experiences of people. For parents of a miscarried baby, a central concern is that the existence of the baby they mourn may go unrecognised. Often the loss is more complicated because there is no recognisable body to see. There is also the difficulty, specific to miscarriage, that at this early stage of pregnancy loss, there is usually the absence of a social support network and rituals, which can normally be available to mourners. At present there are few accepted rituals for mourning an early pregnancy loss. The traditional rituals, such as wakes and funerals, may be considered inappropriate for an early miscarriage.

Mothers may also have to cope with subsequent medical procedures. In the case of an ectopic pregnancy there is the attendant trauma of having to have major surgery to save the mother's life. An attitude does exist that says 'Forget about the baby' or 'You should be grateful to be alive'. Present also is the possible loss, following an ectopic pregnancy, of an ovary, or even loss of fertility. In such cases the loss in miscarriage may not be acknowledged at all.

Against this, it is appropriate to show that, given comparative circumstances, a more sensitive pastoral approach and practice is possible. This practice encourages empathy, acknowledges loss, authenticates grief and validates pain. Within miscarriage itself parents point out how society differentiates between early and late miscarriage in terms of the acknowledgement of the depth of the loss. Research has shown that women who have a miscarriage find it crucial to be given permission to express their feelings. Once granted, the expression of feelings is very intense. For these women it is a great relief to have their feelings accepted as normal.

Stillbirth

'The whole issue of stillborn children and those live borns who die close to birth, the issue of perinatal death, is perhaps most of all a question of human dignity.'[5]

Some of the common causes of stillbirth are:

- Genetic or chromosomal abnormalities
- Complications from pre-eclampsia (toxaemia)
- Placental abruption or when placenta separates from baby
- Complications of umbilical cord compression
- Diabetes in mother
- Domestic violence

Other factors that have been identified include the exposure of the father to radiation, which causes damage to the father's germ cell.[6] Some research has also pointed to a link with low birth weight and a secondary link has been made to smoking. Other research has shown that prospective risk of stillbirth was elevated in certain ethnic groups and revealed increasing significance with advanced maternal age, multiple gestations and lack of prenatal care.[7]

Only in approximately 40 per cent of cases can the cause of the stillbirth be established. Of those for whom a cause can be found, approximately 75 per cent are related to the development of the baby and 25 per cent are related to difficulties with the placenta/umbilical cord. Where this is the case, it can add greatly to the concerns when a mother is pregnant again.

A stillbirth is two separate events: a birth and a death. Lovell (1995) noted that because these two events seem to occur simultaneously, 'life and death seem to collide'.[8] In such a collision there may well be a double impact. Lovell found that some health professionals often behaved as if one cancelled out the other. The obvious risk in such a case is that these experiences of bereaved women may be treated almost as insignificant. A central approach for the best care of those bereaved by stillbirth is achieved by making the most of what is available and can be remembered. In comparison to less helpful approaches, it allows and indeed encourages that a stillborn baby be held, cradled, photographed, named and buried by the parents. Such greater attachment allows more manifest memories to evolve and be treasured.

The nature of loss

> 'First, and usually foremost, perinatal death is a loss of part of the self.'[9]

It has been shown how strong the bonds of attachment are between the parents and child as parents approach the birth of their baby. The emotional turmoil following the death of the baby can be dramatic, diverse and of considerable duration. Some of the initial emotions experienced can be:

- Shock and numbness
- Searching and yearning
- Guilt
- Blame and anger
- Loss of self-esteem
- Envy and jealousy – very painful when in the company of newborn babies and their mothers
- Depression

Associated to these emotions is a diversity of losses:

- Of self-esteem
- Of competence – the ability to be a mother
- Of the experience of pregnancy
- Of anticipated motherhood
- Of special attention
- Of prenatal medical care

It is crucial for those in the caring professions to acknowledge the range of losses involved and the implications for the care-providers. There is a need for clear, empathic responses.

A number of phases have been identified by many writers of grief theory. As already mentioned, such phases are different in each case in terms both of intensity and duration.

Protest
This initial stage of mourning may last for a number of days and is characterised by shock, numbness and disbelief. Difficulties in making decisions can occur and manic episodes may also be present. At this time, anger and hostility may be part of the initial experience of mourning. This anger may be directed towards medical staff, clergy and others working within the hospital setting. It may also be directed upon the parents themselves as they blame themselves for the loss of their baby.

Disorganisation
At this phase the reality of the finality of the loss has been acknowledged and this can be a very painful experience. It may be characterised by searching and yearning for the lost baby. At the same time there may be a withdrawal from the world outside, which may be expressed in losing interest in previously important issues, e.g. loss of interest in food or personal appearance. There can be a preoccupation with thoughts of the

baby. Many parents are aware of personal concerns for their own sanity. A phrase often heard is: 'Am I going crazy?'

Reorganisation
In this phase the bereaved parents start to engage again with the world. It is a time when the memories begin to be less painful and new activities and relationships begin. This new beginning may be coupled with guilt about enjoying life again. Some parents speak about feeling disloyal to the memory of their baby by enjoying things again. It becomes easier to talk about the baby. A phrase used to describe this phase is 'the new normal', an acknowledgement that things are not as they were.

What loss may be like for a mother
There can be a devastating loss of self-esteem with associated feelings of inadequacy and failure. The death of her baby affects a mother's sense of control. Parents see a child as an expression of unrealised omnipotence and so the death of the child attacks their sense of power. Emotional numbness and denial mark the initial phase of maternal grief. It can become nearly impossible to concentrate or make decisions. The language of 'it was like a dream' is frequently heard. There is shock, even when the loss is anticipated, as parents hear silence rather than the cry of their baby.

Mothers have spoken of strong feelings of searching and yearning to hold and nurse their child. Some have expressed their fear of losing their mind as they go through very strong emotional outbursts and crying. Mothers also speak of arms aching to hold their babies. Blame and anger frequently follow and this can be associated with feelings of guilt: 'What did I do wrong?' Women, and at times their partners, may wonder if any of their actions may have led to the death of the baby. Drinking too much alcohol, lifting heavy objects, sex late in pregnancy and working too long into the pregnancy may be seen as reasons to blame oneself. Many researchers see this as a response to the helplessness of the situation. Envy and jealously towards other pregnant women may well occur. This has been linked to feelings of profound inferiority because of a failure to procreate, which can be increased in the presence of other mothers and their babies.

Some writers have drawn attention to the special problems of the mother of a stillborn baby. Because of society's 'abhorrence' to a stillbirth, she is likely to feel avoided by her doctor, her husband and friends. She tends to isolate herself because of her own feelings of failure, and because of shame and guilt that her thoughts or actions might have caused the death. Some researchers have concentrated upon the uniqueness of this death, the loss of a fantasised person who was to be, rather than of a consciously known person. Resolution of this loss varied from person to person. For some mothers, loss of a baby can be seen in terms of the interruption or broken connection of the family generations. Such losses are therefore increasingly complex in resolution. Often the experiences and attitudes of a grandmother or a mother-in-law who previously had a stillbirth may dominate the recently bereaved mother.

Often the bereaved mother may be removed from the whole death process by the administration of sedatives and bland clichés such as 'You can always have another baby'. Pregnancy loss is very much as Leon (1993) defined it, as 'a crisis within a crisis', and it creates a unique type of bereavement. In addition to standard grief that mothers face, this loss can be seen as developmental interference, disrupting what was expected to be a significant event. Such loss sets a bereaved mother apart from many of her friends and family.

Peppers & Knapp (1980), using subjective self-report questionnaires, found that mothers who had lost babies through miscarriage, stillbirth and neonatal death, demonstrated similarity in grief responses. Sometimes it has been expressed that the health services and other agencies believe that the earlier the pregnancy failed, the 'lesser' the loss. This could be seen to imply that miscarriage is less sad than stillbirth; and stillbirth less sad than losing a baby who had lived. Such a grading of losses is unhelpful and ignores the uniqueness of each loss.

Mourning someone who has lived and then dies requires a painful recollection of the past memories relating to that person. This difficult process helps with grief resolution. However, in the case of a perinatal death, there is an inability to recall the fantasies of what was to be, in the absence of a living baby. Such losses are lonely and solitary. Humphrey & Zimpfer (1996) write: 'These losses have been called lonely, because often the mother has been left to grieve the death of her child alone. Often parents must say goodbye to their child before they even say hello'.[10]

Loss for a father

Oh you, core of your father's being,
Light of joy, extinguished too soon![11]

Following a miscarriage or stillbirth, many fathers can feel isolated and left out of what is happening, with their needs being ignored. Part of this is rooted in differences between males and females in their expression of grief. Men do not have different processes of grief from those experienced by women. However, gender-role conditioning has major implications for the way grief is expressed. Men have been brought up and encouraged to control their feelings. Instead of verbalising feelings such as loss, men tend to act them out. Differences between male and female expressions of grief can lead to deep-rooted problems. Women tend to be more open with their feelings and can express them with less difficulty than men. Professor Tom O'Dowd notes how our conditioning helps men and women to get through day-to-day living. However, 'if there is crisis with a strong psychological component, men's conditioning and society's expectations seem to let them down'.[12]

Men tend to be more stoic and less expressive, but what is expressed may well be angrier. Men tend to be more task-orientated; fathers tend to ask the factual questions: why, how and will it ever occur again? With regard to sex, men may see it as a means of expressing intimacy, whereas women may want a non-sexual intimacy.

Research shows that fathers-to-be pass through characteristic stages of expectant fatherhood, which include deep emotional involvement and commitment. Lower level of attachment to the baby has been suggested as an explanation for why men consistently demonstrate lower acute grief scores than women after pregnancy loss. Interestingly, men show higher scores than women on measures of anger, aggression and denial. Grief scores tend to equalise between couples around twelve months after the loss.

The experience of depression
Depression will be a normal reaction following the loss of a baby. However, in some cases the depression can be more serious and may become a long-term problem, requiring professional help.

Possible symptoms of major depression include:

• A noticeable change in either weight gain or
  weight loss
• Disturbed sleep
• Tiredness
• Loss of interest in what is happening
• Feelings of worthlessness; diminished self-esteem
• Paranoia
• Difficulty with concentration

Research has shown that moderate depression in women after the death of their baby can be rated 20 per cent, scoring 17 or more on the Beck scale. In the case of live births, the figure for mothers who were moderately depressed is 4 per cent. Also noted was that the age of the mother seems to make a difference, with younger women being more depressed than older women. Moscarello's research[13] showed that if perinatal bereavement is not resolved, 25 to 33 per cent may go on to develop clinical depression.

What may happen to the relationship between mother and father?

First and foremost, a couple will express and experience grief differently. This is partly due to society's expectations and to the role to which we have been conditioned by our gender. There are also differences in attachment. A mother may see the baby as part of herself. For a father, the difference is that he experiences the baby in part through what his partner shares with him. Ultimately, the greatest problems appear where there is a lack of mutual support, sharing and communication following the loss. Sharing feelings will help, and sometimes when face-to-face communication is difficult, this may be achieved through sending letters. It has been noted that while a father cannot experience pregnancy biologically, there are many parallels for him with a mother in the psychological journey.

Sometimes a mother may view the calm exterior of a father as diffident, if not callous. There is a risk that as a man connects with his emotions he may become isolated and unable to find someone with whom to share his feelings. He may not wish to upset his partner by raising issues with her for fear of upsetting her. He may feel his needs are being ignored by his partner and also by those providing support to her. Moe (1997)[14] identifies the possible creation of two roles following perinatal loss: a consenter and an experiencer. The consenter will seem able to move along with life rather well, consenting to the loss. The experiencer may continue in the opposite pattern. Moe makes the obvious connection: consenters and experiencers do not peacefully coexist very well in the same household, at least while grieving is occurring.

An absence of mutual support and sharing during grieving contributes significantly to complicated grief following perinatal death. Peppers & Knapp explore sexual relations and highlight that they often suffer because one or both partners is experiencing an obsession with becoming pregnant or experiencing guilt about overt pleasure. Studies show that the best adaptation to this type of loss comes when both parents have similar coping styles and open communication. If a couple can understand gender influences in coping, relationship tensions regarding the perception of dissimilar grieving may be reduced.

Staudacher (1991) has highlighted what she believes are the possible issues for a couple following a perinatal death:

- Differing intimacy and sexual needs
- Differing views about having other children
- Disagreements about methods of child-rearing to be used for the surviving child or children
- Negative reactions to spouse's presence, activities or beliefs[15]

Research has been undertaken about the implications for relationships following the loss of a baby. The results are inconclusive. Some research from the USA expresses a link between increased divorce rates and the death of a baby. Other research shows that at both three and nine months after the death of a baby, the women in the study stated that they had a greater closeness with their partners. In addition, only 10 per cent stated that the loss had created any difficulties in their respective relationships.

In 1982, a survey of fifty couples who had suffered the loss of a child through perinatal death noted that half of the women interviewed stated that the loss of the baby had improved their relations with their husbands.[16] The other half stated that their relations had been unaffected by the bereavement.Other research[17] highlights that mothers identified improved relationships with baby's father by the time of the follow-up appointment as compared to the time before the child's birth. The statistics on separation/divorce in the same research suggest no difference in rates between those bereaved by stillbirth and those who experience a live birth.

Problems may be present if there is an increase in alcohol consumption, increased working hours and an over-involvement in church/group. All these actions are signs of distancing. Bowen, from the family therapy school, suggested that one way we limit anxiety in a relationship is by the introduction of such distancing. Other signs could be a noticeable pattern of doting on other children or a lack of sexual relations. A decreased sex life may well be connected to a loss of confidence or the fear of losing another child. Dealing with the grief can be helped primarily by open communication, which involves sharing feelings with partner, family and friends.

Having another baby

When a couple are considering whether to try for another baby, it is very important to acknowledge that their past and shared experience will play a significant role in shaping the next hoped-for pregnancy. For some couples, there may be issues still to be faced and questions that were never answered following the loss. There may be ambivalence to another pregnancy and there can be many mixed feelings. Anxieties and worries are very normal at this time. The joy and expectations associated with pregnancy may be tinged with many emotions flowing directly from the previous loss: fear, grief, guilt, etc. For many parents, questions concerning subsequent pregnancies are major decisions.

At this stage a couple needs to be aware that another baby will not reduce the grief for their last child, nor can a subsequent baby be a replacement for the baby who died. Consideration may need to be given to the physical health and age of the mother. Communication between the couple is vital, especially if there are differing views on the best timing to try for a baby. For some couples, the need for another baby can border on being an obsession and professional care may well be of help in such cases. In the past, conventional wisdom has advised couples to have another baby as quickly as possible. Recent research[18] reports that vulnerability to depression and anxiety in the next pregnancy and *puerperium* is related to the period of time since stillbirth, with more recently bereaved women at a significantly greater risk. Such research suggests that there may be advantages in waiting a year before the next conception.

Bourne & Lewis (1984) expressed the view that a subsequent pregnancy should be postponed until the main mourning period has passed. The mother cannot complete the mourning process when she becomes preoccupied with her growing baby and the impending birth.[19] Studies consistently report that about 50 per cent of women become pregnant within a year of their loss.[20] On the other hand, Cuisinier et al. (1996)[21] found that bereaved mothers conceiving again lessened grief, and they also noted that a speedy new pregnancy was rarely found to be detrimental. They suggested that parents should no longer be advised to wait a specific time before conceiving again. They advocate that individual situations should be discussed with the medical profession in order to help parents to make an informed decision concerning subsequent pregnancy. The advice offered seems to be: 'Wait until you feel ready and have adjusted to your loss'.

It may be helpful for parents considering trying for another baby, to ask themselves the following two questions:
Am I expecting the next baby to make me feel better?
Does the loss of our baby still occupy all aspects of my life?

Other unique situations to be considered

1. If the baby has died already in utero
Once it has been realised that a baby has already died while still in the womb, a decision has to be made on the timing of delivery. In certain circumstances a standard delivery rather than a section is appropriate. Some recent research suggests that it is advisable to induce the delivery as soon as feasible after the diagnosis.[22] The importance of a calm environment for the mother is seen as crucial, as is the acknowledged need for those providing care to be flexible to the needs of the mother. On occasion, parents have not been helped by the attitude that assumes that an anticipated loss is not as traumatic as an unexpected one.

2. The death of a twin
There are a number of unique aspects present when one baby dies and the other lives. Criticism has been levelled at health-care providers in such cases. Wilson et al. (1982) suggest that even less support than usual appears to be present for the mother. The usual response centres upon the mother's expected gratitude for having a second child who has survived. The research found that the presence of a live baby did not lessen the grieving process, even though friends, family and hospital staff tended to assume that the grief of parents would be lessened. Lewis & Bryan (1988)[23] noted that the death of a twin during pregnancy or around birth gives rise to a bewildering confusion of thoughts and feelings that can impede mourning and can also disturb the bereaved mother's care of the surviving twin. The authors advocate that every effort should be made to give the parents and siblings an experience of the dead baby.

What may help following the death of a twin:

- Be aware of the conflicting emotions. Twins may often be viewed in the womb as one unit.
- Be aware of the pain in celebrating a new life that is conjoined with a death.
- Be aware of the feelings of vulnerability for the surviving twin.
- It is helpful to acknowledge both the death of one twin and the birth of the other. Some parents have achieved this by planting two trees – one for each baby.
- There is a need to guard against the inappropriate comments of third parties: 'Well, at least you have one baby'.
- Consideration should, in time, be given to the issue of birthdays, etc.

At the time of the birth it may help if:

- There are opportunities to hold and view both babies.
- Photographs of the babies are taken together and separately.
- The birth and death are announced simultaneously.
- Mementoes are kept of both babies.

3. When the parents are teenage parents

If a teenager experiences a pregnancy loss there may be additional issues to be addressed. Such a pregnancy is usually unplanned and sometimes the mother may feel guilty for not wanting the baby in the early weeks of the pregnancy. A teenager may also be moving from being dependent upon parents to becoming independent and such a loss may be compounded by the difficulty of self-identification. While physically a teenager may seem like an adult, she may still be lacking in emotional maturity and understanding. Such mothers are often only children themselves.

An additional factor is that there may be no partner present, which may increase the dependency on parents. Often a partner has the role of advocate, and if there is no partner the young mother may feel isolated and voiceless. Those caring need to be aware that there may also be additional losses, with possible relationship difficulties for the young parents. There may be concerns about continuing education. Research has shown that teenage parents may feel that the grief can be got rid of by having another baby as soon as possible.

4. Shadow grief

A unique aspect of perinatal death is shadow grief, which was identified by Peppers & Knapp[24] in 1980. It is a form of lingering and transient sadness, which may still recur years after the loss. It can be seen as a tendency for painful memories and sensations to arise on anniversary dates, such as the stillborn baby's due date and delivery date. It may also connect with the anticipated day when schooling was to commence or with religious rites of passage such as first communion or confirmation. As children born at the same time reach these milestones, the bereaved parents recall their own child and how things could have been. Many theorists link shadow grief to the profound sense of isolation – from hospital staff, community, family and friends – experienced by the bereaved mother. In many such situations, mothers seem to be encouraged to maintain a conspiracy of silence and to resist exploring their feelings publicly.

Tears and a real sense of things not being right can mark the passing of these major events. Some mothers still speak of a sense of isolation and of feelings that other people do not understand their loss. This can feed into the conspiracy of silence, where mothers sense they are not being encouraged to explore or to express their feelings.

5. Bittersweet grief

Bittersweet grief was a term used by Karen Kowlaski and it refers to the presence of memoirs that can cause feelings of both sadness and happiness. As time passes this may increase and it can be very real following the birth of another baby. This experience needs to be acknowledged. Often one of the greatest problems that perpetuate grief is the manner in which other people avoid mentioning the dead baby.

Loss – as a family experience

Brothers and sisters

Stillborn

'Oh! Is that what it means?' he said.
'I thought it meant
He was still born
Even though he was dead.'

(by Siobhán Parkinson,[25] *with acknowledgement to the words of the author's son, Matthew, aged six, when his brother Daniel was stillborn.)*

A miscarriage or stillbirth affects every member of the family, and children are no exception. Cain, Erikson, et al. (1964) noted that miscarriages 'do not occur in a uterus, but in a woman; and … miscarriages do not occur solely in a woman, but in a family'.[26] Children, therefore, must be included in the loss, and this is difficult for parents in the midst of terrible suffering.

How children in a family react to pregnancy loss can be determined first by a child's cognitive development and capacity to understand death. A second factor is the response of the parents, especially the primary caregiver. There is a temptation to avoid explaining what has happened. But children can be intuitive and realise something is not right within the family. What seems most appropriate is a clear and simple explanation. This can help the whole family in coming to terms with the loss. Words need to be chosen carefully and explanations such as 'taken by God' or 'fallen asleep' should be avoided. The use of such language can lead to distorted ideas about illness, death and doctors. Appropriate language for the age of the child must be used in order to avoid excessive fantasies and fears.

Children react individually to loss and they may become vulnerable because they are dependent on the adults in their world. If they sense a withdrawal by their parents, especially their mother, they can feel threatened. As a general rule for those under five years of age, their greatest fear is of being left alone. Children aged between five and nine may understand that death is final but they do not believe it happens to everyone. For those over nine years of age, there is the acceptance that death is inevitable for everyone.

In the past, the loss of a baby has been an invisible loss for the remaining siblings. Children rarely saw their dead brother or sister and their parents often failed to explain their loss. Siblings were also given little opportunity to express their feelings or be part of the funeral ritual.

In deciding whether children should see the baby and attend the funeral, parents tend to be the best judge. Conscious of the emotional pain for parents, it would be helpful to look for guidance from trusted friends or family. Throughout this sad time there must be acknowledgement of how difficult it can be for stressed parents to give the reassurance that their children want. Following a family bereavement the relationships within the family may change, with the other children being viewed as inferior replacements, blameworthy scapegoats, or endangered survivors.

For parents who wish to protect their remaining children from the pain in the family, such powerlessness can be very traumatic. However, Kohner & Henley make the point that parents cannot grieve for their children, or take away their grief or upset.[27]

In caring for children the following characteristics need to be kept in mind:

- Their lack of experience of death.
- Their lack of understanding of the nature of death.
- They may have no words to express emotions and thoughts.
- They may have little control of life.
- They grieve intermittently.
- They need to have reassurance that physical and emotional needs will be met.
- Play does express what is on a child's mind.

What helps when talking to children about death?

- Allow and encourage them to talk about their feelings.
- Talk about the experiences the child has had to date – mother's tummy growing; parents crying; mother in hospital.
- Encourage questions.
- Tell children what to expect.
- Strengthen positive memories.
- Inform the school.

Children and funerals – when is a child old enough to attend?
Things to consider:

- Has the child expressed an interest in attending the funeral?
- Is the child old enough to understand, to some extent, what is happening at a funeral?
- Has the child asked for a discussion about the funeral? Has there been time to celebrate and remember life, a time for the family members to help each other?

Preparation that will help:

- Describe what will happen in the church/crematorium beforehand.
- Tell the children that people may be sad, especially those who normally provide stability.
- Tell them it is all right to cry.
- Ask the child/children if they would like to see the baby.
- Try to have a sensitive and supportive person, who is not overwhelmed with loss, available at all times to help.
- Explore, at an appropriate time, the reasons why a child does not wish to attend.

Grandparents and extended family
In the face of the loss of a child, it is not just the siblings who are deeply affected; grandparents may be victims of a double pain, having experienced the loss of a grandchild while at the same time seeing their children suffer. Just as parents have their hopes wiped out, the same loss of hope is experienced by grandparents.

Grandparents have a very important role as supporters for their children. Often it is grandparents who use the baby's name most frequently and in the process give value to their dead grandchild. It is worth remembering that:

- Expectations and plans made by grandparents for their grandchildren will not be met. Grandparents' feelings may not be acknowledged or met.
- Their grief may connect with previous losses. One needs to be aware if a grandmother has suffered the death of a baby, especially if she reacts stoically.
- Grandparents may have difficulties in understanding grief.

Notes:

1. Reprinted with permission from RTS *Bereavement Training in Pregnancy Loss and Newborn Death* (2001), Bereavement Services, Gundersen Lutheran Medical Foundation: La Crosse, WI, US).

2. Klaus, J.H., Kennell, J. H. & Klaus, P.H., *Bonding: Building the Foundations of Secure Attachment and Independence* (Perseus Press, New York, 1996).

3. Mitchell, K. & Anderson, H., *All our Losses, All our Griefs* (Westminster Press, Philadelphia, 1983), p.57.

4. Allen, M. & Marks, S., *Miscarriage; Women sharing from the heart* (John Wiley & Sons, New York, 1993).

5. Wretmark, A.A., *Perinatal Death as a Pastoral Problem* (Almqvist & Wiksell International, Stockholm, 1993), p.26.

6. Parker et al., 'Stillbirths among offspring of male radiation workers at Sellafield nuclear reprocessing plant' in *Lancet*, Vol. 354, 1999.

7. Feldman, G.B., 'Prospective risk of stillbirth' in *Obstet Gynecol* 80, No. 3, Pt. 1, 1992 pp.473-4.

8. Lovell, A., *A Bereavement with a Difference* (South Bank University, London, 1995), p.8.

9. Leon I., *When a Baby Dies: Psychotherapy for Pregnancy and Newborn Loss* (Yale University Press, New Haven, 1990), p.39.

10. Humprey, G. & Zimpfer, D., *Counselling for Grief & Bereavement* (Sage Publications, London, 1996), p.142.

11. Ruckert, F., *Kindertotenlieder – Songs on the Death of Children* (poems set to music by Gustav Mahler).

12. O'Dowd, T., 'The Needs of Fathers' in *British Medical Journal* 306, 1993, pp.184-5.

13. Moscarello, R., 'Perinatal bereavement support services: three year review' in *Journal of Palliative Care* 5(4), 1989, pp.12-18.

14. Moe, T., *Pastoral Care in Pregnancy Loss* (Haworth Press, New York, 1997).

15. Staudacher, C., *Men & Grief* (New Harbinger Publications, California, 1991), p.136.

16. Forest, C. G., Standish, E., & Baun, J.D., *Support after Perintal Death: a study of support and counselling after perinatal bereavement.* British Medical Journal 285:1982 pp. 1475-8.

17. Radestad et al., 'Stillbirth and maternal well being' in *Acta Obstet Gynecol Scan*, Oct.: 76, 1997.

18. Hughes, P.M., Turton, P., Evans, C.D.H., 'Stillbirth as risk factor for depression and anxiety in the subsequent pregnancy: cohort study' in *British Medical Journal* 318, 2000, pp.17-21.

19. Bourne, S. & Lewis, E., 'Delayed psychological effects of perinatal deaths; the next pregnancy and the next generation' in *British Medical Journal* 289, 1984, p.148.

20. Forrest, G.C. et al., 'Support after perinatal death' in *British Medical Journal* 285, 1982, pp.1475-9.

21. Cuisiner et al., 'Pregnancy following miscarriage: course of grief and some determining factors' in *Journal Psychosomatic Obstetric Gynaecology* 17(3), 1996, pp.163-8.

22. Radestad, I. et al., 'Psychological complications after stillbirth – influence of memories and immediate management: population based study' in *British Medical Journal* 312, 1996, pp.1505-08.

23. Lewis, E. & Bryan, E., ' Management of perinatal death of a twin' in *British Medical Journal* 297, 1988, pp.1321-3.

24. Knapp, R., & Peppers, L., 'Doctor-patient relationships in foetal/infant death encounters' in *Journal of Medical Education* 54, Oct. 1979, pp.775-80.

25. Parkinson, S., from *A Part of Ourselves* (A & A Farmer, Dublin, 1997), p.122.

26. Cain, Erikson et al., 'Children's disturbed reactions to their mother's miscarriage' in *Psychosomatic Medicine* 26(1), 1964, pp.58-66.

27. Kohner, N. & Henley, A., *When a Baby Dies* (Pandora Press, London, 1991), p.103.

5
The Caring Professions

Research has shown consistently the crucial importance of those in the caring professions as they help bereaved parents. Constantly improving standards and insight into appropriate responses have assisted parents following their baby's death. This chapter proposes an overview in this regard. Essentially, it will explore the roles of those in the caring professions who provide immediate and follow-up care to bereaved families. The contributions of the medical and nursing professions, together with clergy, will be addressed.

For those in the caring professions it is important to assess the nature, extent and feelings of parents who have experienced pregnancy loss. Consideration should always be given to prevalent research, e.g. that by Allen & Marks 1993. Important issues in the process of assessment include an analysis of any past history of pregnancy, and particularly pregnancy loss. Central in this regard is how losses were viewed and experienced by the parents.

Following the death of a baby it is important that any response from the caring professions be appropriate and measured. Essentially, this means that they must continue to offer choices. This should always be coupled with gentleness and appropriate timing. There is a very definite role here for an inter/multidisciplinary team approach. The advantages of such an approach are twofold. First, it gives an holistic and ongoing response to parents and family; second, it allows different professions to support each other and thereby guard against the possibility of burnout. Such a team approach necessarily presupposes a prevailing mindset; it requires collaboration, consultation and regular reviews.

Medical profession

In the past, the medical profession has come in for criticism regarding the care offered to parents following the death of their baby. This stems in part from the method and perception amongst authors in the 1950s and 1960s, which effectively demonstrated a lack of awareness that miscarriage could have a serious psychological impact on a woman. Cain et al. (1964) were the first to offer an alternative perspective, noting how miscarriage had been almost consistently viewed as an isolated medical problem and, as such, had been almost consistently treated in a mechanical and physical manner. Parents whose baby was lost early in the pregnancy tended to express greater dissatisfaction with their medical care. Bereaved parents expressed anger at treatment from hospital staff, who had seemed reluctant to recognise and respond to a loss that was perceived as less important than that of a stillborn baby. An ongoing concern for some mothers who have had a number of miscarriages is that multiple miscarriages are not investigated until at least three have occurred in sequence.

Another problem in the past was the lack of communication between the medical staff and the bereaved parents. Research from the 1970s noted that 60 per cent of mothers, following prenatal death, felt extremely dissatisfied with the available information. Part of the problem seems to have been that two languages were being used. Sometimes it seemed as if the medical terminology – miscarriage, spontaneous abortion, and the inviability of the foetus – was not connected to the feelings of the parents. There are still some real difficulties as medical criteria and definitions are applied with inappropriateness to the grief of the parents. For some medical professionals, there is a tendency to compare one kind of loss with another. For some parents, such comparisons are meaningless.

Kohner & Henley wrote in 1991 that parents know only what they have experienced, which is loss, and that cannot, and should not, be categorised.[1] For some bereaved parents, ill feeling has been rooted in the withholding of medical foreknowledge. There is a suggestion that some professionals may have failed to support parents because they lack the imagination to feel what another person is feeling. Other professionals do not understand because they themselves have not experienced anything that would help them to understand.[2]

It should be acknowledged that the experience of loss introduces one to the whole area of personal mortality and vulnerability. Paradoxically, this is an area that many healthcare professionals studiously try to avoid. Some have adopted an attitude of 'unemotional professionalism', which may well serve to block their own grief and the sense of loss in terms of their efficacy following the death of a baby. Research has shown that patients who received personal, ongoing follow-up from their physicians, were considerably more likely to be satisfied with the nature and type of information provided and the care they received. The centrality of good, clear communication with parents is crucial.

Increasingly, the medical profession has acknowledged the extent and nature of parental grief by including sections within paediatric and obstetric textbooks. Medical protocols have been developed and refined in the case of perinatal loss. Kennell et al. (1970), Connolly (1982) O'Dowd (1993) and many other members of the medical profession have, in their time, written extensively on the real needs of bereaved parents. Recommendations and suggestions have been made for their peers, hospital management and for all those involved in the healthcare professions. In recent guidelines from the Royal College of Obstetrics and Gynaecology (RCOG), the following pointers have been made for carers following perinatal death:

- Parents and family should be offered privacy in a private room.
- Parents should be given the choice of being on or off the post-natal ward.
- Parents should be given every opportunity to see their baby.
- Literature from various support groups should be available to the parents.

In similar publications, the RCOG suggests that 'patients should be treated with courtesy and respect at all times. Medical staff should take as a model how they themselves would like to be treated, or those they care about, such as their mother, daughter or partner'. Attitudes have certainly changed. In two surveys in Scandinavia (1989 and 1994) researchers noted an improvement in the perceived care by mothers following loss, from 68 per cent to 95 per cent. This was based upon increased support and counselling.

What the medical profession can do to assist parents in their loss
In a compilation of previously written material and personal research, the following list sets out what parents have expressed as being most helpful in their loss:

- Inform both parents, if possible, of the bad news.
- Offer clear communication, without using clichés.
- Use language that is understood by the parents.
- Check that the parents clearly understand the situation.
- Be aware of the possible issues of guilt, blame and anger.
- Be aware that every word and gesture is open to interpretation.

- Be available for extended conversation: the initial meeting may not be the time for lengthy explanations.
- Use the word 'baby' rather than 'foetus'.
- Be aware of the practical issues, e.g. lactation.

Nursing/midwife profession

It is those in the nursing profession who tend to spend the greatest amount of time with bereaved parents. As with the clergy, a nurse/midwife may well have built up a relationship with the parents as the pregnancy progressed. Following the death of a baby, the midwife has a crucial role in ensuring that all that can be done for the parents and the baby is achieved.

The midwife will make a nursing assessment of the situation. An important function is to clarify both what the parents know and what they understand. The midwife may well act as an interpreter, if necessary, ensuring that whatever medical terminology has been used is comprehended. This may take quite a while. Also, the midwife will take into account the cultural and religious needs of the family and will link them with pastoral care and social work as necessary.

The midwife may also act as the link person between various groups and may be the person who ensures that all family members are contacted. As time progresses it may be the midwife who encourages all those actions that will help – giving permission to cradle the baby, to take photographs, etc. For many parents the most positive aspect in their loss has been the ongoing support and professional care that they have received from members of the nursing profession.

Pastoral/spiritual care
Presence means

> *Be near, but don't hover.*
> *DON'T JUST DO SOMETHING! STAND THERE!*
> *Don't fill silence with talk.*
> *Don't give answers to questions that have no answers.*
> *Deal with your own anxiety and sadness.*
> *Don't assume what you should do – Ask!*
> *Let your heart do the talking – not your head.*
> *Speak to feelings – not the words.*
> *('Why did this happen' – the feeling is despair; address*
> *that.)*
> *Encourage hoping carefully.*
> *Encourage people to make their own meaning of the*
> *experience.* [3]

Some clergy[4] have come in for criticism in terms of the appropriateness of their care. Research in the USA by Cunningham in 1983 highlighted that only half of the clergy were seen to be understanding and supportive following the death of a baby. Congregations were seen as even less responsive, with only a third regarded as helpful. More recent research would increase the positive percentages but many stories can still be heard of unhelpful churches and clergy. Thomas Moe highlighted how clergy[5] prioritised their responses in terms of the age of the baby:

Clergy responses to loss based on age of child

Type of Loss	Times considered not worthy of ministry
Miscarriage	24.6% of respondents
Baby	10.2% of respondents
Four-year-old child	6.3% of respondents
Twelve-year-old child	4.9% of respondents

Lovell, writing in 1997[6] about the UK situation, highlights a view that clergy seem slow to change their practice with regard to prenatal death. One possible cause is explored in the ongoing patriarchal system of the Church. Like Wretmark, Lovell notes how groups are now developing their own rituals, independent of the institutional Church. Bereaved parents encounter clergy either in their role as chaplain to a hospital, or as house clergy. Often mothers who have miscarried may not see the chaplain, as their stay could be very short. The relationship between a chaplain and the local clergy is an important one. Often bereaved parents may have little contact with local clergy, and the chaplain, subject to the wishes of the couple, may initiate contact and in turn follow-up with the local clergy.

Clergy have a number of roles following the death of a baby. Crucially, clergy must be aware that such grief can be belittled – as Cunningham notes: 'It may be a LITTLE baby, but it is a big GRIEF'.[7] There is the immediate trauma following the death, which requires appropriate care. Clergy may be one of the few groups that have already established a long-term relationship with the parents. This is often cross-generational and the minister may care for three generations at the same time. Such rapport can be of enormous assistance in a time of great loss. In the immediate aftermath of a death, parents have commented on how they have valued the presence of clergy. Limbo & Wheeler describe the clergy's role in terms of an intimate carer: 'a participant rather than an observer'.[8]

Clergy also have a role in marking the ritual of the beginning and ending of life. They can initiate and help parents with funeral arrangements. (Suggestions on how a service may be enhanced can be found later in this book.) As with the nursing and social-work professions, clergy may undertake the role of advocate. In such cases the silent voices of the bereaved parents may be given strong voice when necessary. The clergy, social workers or midwife may become the link person for the family, liaising with the funeral directors, etc. It is important to have good and supportive relationships between the different healthcare professionals.

With the bereaved parents, many faith questions may be raised. Those in ministry must be sensitive to the differences that may exist between their own theology and that of the parents. Different spiritualities must be respected and honoured. Clergy need to be sensitive to the fact that parents may come from different traditions, or may have different understandings while sharing the same tradition. There is a need for awareness that there can be a large difference between a person's denominational label and their personal beliefs. The death of a baby may evoke guilt and such emotions need great amounts of time. Often the prime role for clergy is to listen to the story, sometimes repeatedly. Following a death, it is not unusual for issues around meaning and well-trusted faith formulae to be presented and challenged. The death encounter is, for many, the first real experience of spiritual encounter and spiritual brokenness. The parents' relationship with and understanding of God will often be confronted and even shattered. Clergy must also be aware that the raising of such issues may well, in themselves, cause feelings of guilt for parents. There is a need to be aware that religion, upbringing and faith tradition have implications for our understanding of death and for issues surrounding the death of a child, such as baptism and limbo.

Clergy also have an important role in providing follow-up care. In addition, they can encourage their congregation to offer care too, and can provide information on the various support groups. Parents have commented on how, in time, they have appreciated the link-up with other parents who have lost a child.

In this chapter, the importance of the relative healthcare professionals has been explored. In the next chapter, a wider reflection on what really helps parents in their grief will be offered.

Notes:

1. Kohner, N. & Henley, A., *When a Baby Dies* (Pandora Press, London, 1991), p.64.
2. Ibid.
3. Based upon a lecture 'The role of clergy in perinatal loss' by Rev. Mary Harrison, 12 September 1990. Used with permission.
4. The term clergy in the text refers to the prime spiritual provider – lay or ordained.
5. Moe, T., *Pastoral Care in Pregnancy Loss* (Howarth Press, New York, 1997), p.15.
6. Lovell, A., 'Death at the beginning of life' in *Death, Gender and Ethnicity* (Routledge, London, 1997), p.46.
7. Cunningham in Woods & Woods, *Loss During Pregnancy or in the Newborn Period* (Janetti Publications, New Jersey, 1997), p.491.
8. Limbo, R. & Wheeler, S., *When a Baby Dies: A Handbook for Healing and Helping* (Lutheran Hospital, La Crosse, Wisconsin, 1986), p.142.

6
What Really Helps the Bereaved

What Do You Say?

What do you say when a baby dies and someone says ...
> *'At least you didn't bring it home'.*

What do you say when a baby is stillborn and someone says ...
> *'At least it never lived'.*

What do you say when a mother of three says ...
> *'Think of all the time you'll have'.*

What do you say when so many say ...
> *'You can always have another ... '*
> *'At least you never knew it ... '*
> *'You have your whole life ahead of you ...'*
> *'You have an angel in heaven'.*

What do you say when someone says ... nothing?

What do you say when someone says...
> *'I'm sorry'.*

You say, with grateful tears and warm embrace,
> *'Thank You!'*

Kathie Rataj Mayo[1]

' ... *the most important action is to listen, listen and listen
some more.*'[2]

Reflecting on their experiences of bereavement, parents often
identify three common ways in which people respond to them.
The first way is where people avoid any mention of the loss.
This response possibly stems from a belief that a conversation
will only reopen the wounds. Such action may come from an
inability to stay with pain or tears. A second possible reaction
resounds with inappropriateness and insensitivity. This is the
stage at which the clichés appear: 'you can always have another
one; you have an angel in heaven; it was for the best'. Such
clichés do little to help those bereaved. The third approach is
the path of compassion and empathy. This is an approach of
listening to the story, many times if necessary, and of simply
saying, 'I'm sorry'. Many parents have commented on how they
valued the request to tell their story about their baby.

With that in mind, the purpose of this chapter is to look at
what can be helpful to bereaved parents and their families.

The role of the professional
Research has shown that supportive counselling by a well-trained
multidisciplinary team greatly helps parents. In a hospital setting
there is a crucial role for the individual carer, be it a midwife, social
worker or chaplain. The professional carer has tasks of listening,
anticipating needs, offering options and helping the parents to get
some control over their lives. Of course, all this must be done in
an appropriate manner. There is a need to acknowledge the
specific religious, cultural and ethnic situation of the family, and
to facilitate them in making their own decisions.

In the short term, professional care has a crucial role in
helping to build up the memories of the baby and to facilitate the
appropriate ritual. In the long term, there may be a role in
helping the parents to consider having other children and being
available to explore the issues of infertility if they arise. Many

professional carers have found the use of checklists very important.

What helps parents in the short term?
One of the hardest tasks facing bereaved parents is that they must prepare to say goodbye before they have said hello. The following list sets out what parents have acknowledged as being of help to them in their loss.

- Freedom of choice.
- Time to name their baby.
- The opportunity to express their feelings whenever necessary.
- Time to hold and cradle their baby.
- Time to be with their baby.
- Having an appropriate place to be with the baby.
- The saving and collecting of all that is connected to their baby, including mementoes:
  - Baby's wristband and umbilical clip.
  - Footprint, handprint, lock of hair, pictures.
  - The baby's blanket, toys.
- The opportunity to have a ritual of naming or blessing.
- Being provided with information and contact with the support groups.
- Not being rushed into putting away things that were set aside for the baby.
- Communicating with local clergy if required.
- Being allowed to ask questions as often as necessary, and being given appropriate answers.
- Support in making final arrangements: liaising with the undertaker; making sure everything is done correctly; transporting the baby if necessary; an explanation of the post-mortem procedure.
- Being given anything that acknowledges their baby's existence, for example, blessing cards.

- Follow-up care, especially on anniversaries and other special family days.
- The breaking of the conspiracy of silence that hampers the grieving process in families.

Many questions are raised as soon as parents realise that their baby is dead. Space and time must be given for these to be asked and often repeated. Research has shown that the most common questions raised are:[3]

- Why did this happen?
- God, why did this happen?
- Am I losing my mind?
- Should we have another child?
- How long will the pain last?
- Should I reach out for help?

What may help if you have been bereaved?

- Keep communicating with your partner, family and friends. Keep telling the story.
- Avail of the various support groups, when the time seems right.
- Take care of your physical health, avoid alcohol and tobacco, and make sure you have good nutrition, exercise and rest. Keep follow-up appointments.
- Write a journal.
- Limit changes.
- Be open to help from others.

Role of friends and family
Research has shown the undeniable value of friends and relatives in helping those who have undergone trauma. Many bereaved parents welcome friends who do not try to avoid the sadness of the loss, nor provide clichés or quick fixes to the

pain. Parents have commented on how they really valued their
friends who simply said: 'I just do not know what to say, but I
am so sorry that this happened to you'. Friends have often been
the people who have provided the special mementoes following
the death of a baby. For example, when their friends, near the
anniversary of their baby's death, brought them to a forest
where a tree had been planted in their baby's name.

Holding and seeing the baby

Extensive research emphasises that the contact between parents
and their dead baby holds significant and considerable import,
namely, the reality of the baby's life and the reality of its death.
It is a couple's one chance to be with their baby, to experience
some bonding and to create memories that will one day be
cherished. It is essential to prepare the family before they see
and hold the baby, especially if there is bruising or other visible
marks on the baby. Some authors have suggested that there is a
potential for danger in idealising a dead child when ambivalent
feelings are denied. Other children born subsequently, cannot
match up to the 'good' dead baby who never cried or
demanded, in contrast to the living child who demands and
may have been conceived as a replacement.

A fundamental requirement of the grieving process is the
establishment of memories. Moreover, such memories, be they
fantasies or actual memories, become more tangible when they
take the form of the dead baby's body. Interacting with the
dead baby – seeing, touching, cradling, kissing and sharing –
may facilitate mourning in different ways. Leon (1990) suggests
that viewing the dead baby also facilitates the resolving of the
narcissistic loss – by seeing one's self reflected in one's child,
one is more able to mourn the part of oneself that has been
lost.[4]

Seeing a dead baby can offset the sense of helplessness
engendered by the loss. Time spent holding a dead baby creates
indelible memories, which will be recalled again and again in

the future. By linking the mother's feelings and wishes for her fantasised baby with what she is cradling in her arms, she may be better able to grieve. Engaging with their dead baby also helps fathers in their grief. In addition, it is important for the family and friends to see the baby. This connects them and also helps parents to talk about their baby afterwards.

Many researchers on perinatal loss have described the intense yearning of the bereaved mother for physical contact with her dead child. Most grieving is by nature retrospective, looking back over the full years of memories. When a baby dies at birth parents commence to let go their hopes and fantasies for their child, but they do so in the absence of any memories of their living child.

Photography

Photographs are very important memories that parents can treasure. Many parents can show photographs of their baby and it can be part of the process of validating their role as parents. In the sharing of photographs parents are able to share the story of their baby. Many parents will treasure the positive comments that such photographs will evoke.

Photographs also help to put imagination at rest and reassure parents that they will not forget what their baby was like. The question often appears as to when photographs can be taken. Many parents who have miscarried early have treasured the photographs taken of their baby. I know of one colleague who facilitated this, in the case of an early miscarriage, with the use of an appropriate small jewellery box.

It is useful to be aware that Polaroid photographs may fade over time and that it may be best to use either a 35mm or digital camera. There is great scope in taking such photographs and anything that will link parents with their baby will be very useful. A treasured memory could be a photograph of both parents' wedding rings on the baby's wrist.

Follow-up

Follow up is a crucial part of the care of those bereaved. Parents often have a fear that their baby will be forgotten and, therefore, ongoing visits help greatly. Various time frames have been suggested. The RTS Programme recommended the following time frames:

Following miscarriage:

- Within one week
- Between three weeks and four months
- At the due date or anniversary date

Following stillbirth:

- Within one week
- At three weeks
- At four months
- At due date
- Six to ten months
- Anniversary date

Complicated grief

On occasion, the grief following the loss of a baby becomes complicated grief. Possible symptoms of this prolonged grief may be:

- A continuing dependency upon alcohol or medication.
- Continuous sleeping problems.
- Being totally absorbed in work – this is more prevalent in men.
- Major and continuing changes in weight loss or gain.
- Becoming isolated from friends and family and other relationship problems.
- When the loss always raises great emotional pain, even after a considerable time has passed.

- Continuing thoughts of suicide.
- Turning inwards, with no enthusiasm for life.

In such cases professional care may be crucial in order for the bereaved to move on.

Woods & Woods (1997) set out the following as factors associated with the intensity of grief:

- Previous poor adjustment following the death of infant.
- Loss of a planned pregnancy.
- Not seeing the baby.
- Marital problems.
- Presence of a surviving twin.
- Subsequent pregnancy less than five months after the loss.

In this chapter the importance of appropriate and sensitive care was explored together with various guidelines and suggestions. In the next chapter we will look specifically at the importance of ritual for the bereaved family.

Notes:

1. Reprinted with permission from RTS *Bereavement Training in Pregnancy Loss and Newborn Death* (2001), (Bereavement Services, Gundersen Lutheran Medical Foundation: La Crosse, WI, US).
2. Kennell, J. & Klaus, M., *Maternal Infant Bonding* (C.V. Mosby, St Louis, 1976), p.259.
3. DeFrain, J., 'Learning about grief from normal families: SIDS, stillbirth and miscarriage' in *Journal of Marital and Family Therapy* 17(3), 1991, pp.215-32.
4. Leon, I., *When a Baby Dies – Psychotherapy for Pregnancy and Newborn Loss* (Yale University Press, New Haven, 1990), p.44.

7
Rituals – Funerals, Prayers and Practice

For a child born dead

What ceremony can we fit
you into now? If you had come
out of a warm and noisy room
to this, there'd be an opposite
for us to know you by. We could
imagine you in lively mood.

And then look at the other side,
the mood drawn out of you, the breath
defeated by the power of death.
But we have never seen you stride
ambitiously the world we know.
You could not come and yet you go.

But there is nothing now to mar
your clear refusal of our world.
Not in our memories can we mould
you or distort your character.
Then all our consolation is
that grief can be as pure as this.

Elizabeth Jennings

Research shows that having some ritual can help parents, and the family, following the death of their baby. Ritual, through the use of symbols, gestures, music and words, allows for the expression of those feelings and experiences for which mere words sometimes cannot be found. The main functions or meanings of rituals are:

- They offer a sense of identity, of 'we-ness', which cements the bonds among members of a particular group.
- They offer to participants a sense of living in a regular, reliable, trustworthy world.
- They symbolise in many cases a deeply felt reality, a truth about God or self or life.

In the situation of the death of a baby, ritual helps families to:

- Acknowledge and affirm the life and death of their precious child;
- Continue the process of building up memories;
- Remember, even if the memories are very scarce;
- Start the grief journey.

The rituals of the Christian Church
Nowadays, there is a greater flexibility in approach to a specific pastoral need. In the area of liturgical response to the tragedy of miscarriage and stillbirth, there is evidence of new and innovative approaches. These losses are now seen as real losses necessitating an appropriate and full liturgical response to acknowledge what has occurred. Value and worth are now properties connected with such loss.

If changes occur whereby stillborn babies are now perceived to be of great value, then developments will occur in all aspects pertaining to the reverent care of the baby and the pastoral response to the bereaved parents.

Liturgy within the Anglican Communion
There is diversity within the Anglican Communion reflecting different cultural understandings. During the 1980s, liturgical revision took place on a wide scale throughout the Anglican Communion, moving liturgy beyond the standard *Book of Common Prayer* (1662). In the Church of Ireland, a new one-page liturgy was approved in 1987, entitled 'After the delivery of a still-born child or the death of a newly born child'. This new liturgy offered a set of prayers, a commendation and some proposed psalms. On reflection, this liturgy was not sufficient, if its role was to show that there was a full acceptance of a stillborn or unbaptised child into the Church or acceptance of the child as a full human being.

A further revision in Church of England liturgy (1989) reviewed and extended the liturgy with the following title: 'Funeral service for a child dying near the time of birth'. This extended liturgical resource was eight pages long, with a three-page commentary. An important factor of this new liturgy was that for the first time, a full funeral service for a stillborn baby or a baby who has died soon after birth, was established and made acceptable. The provision of a full funeral service gave value to the sense of loss experienced by parents. The commentary said clearly that a stillborn baby could only be spoken of in terms of a human being.

Concern was expressed that the language was too theological for many bereaved parents who had little contact with Church life. Interviews undertaken with chaplains reveal that a set liturgy may, on occasion, be considered inappropriate. The majority of chaplains have their own liturgy, which is redesigned and reworked before each service. The Church of England's *Common Worship* (2000) also set out a two-page theological reflection, again affirming some of the issues raised in 1989.

Within the wider Anglican Communion there is great diversity, with some useful resources, especially from *A Prayer Book of Australia* (1995). In an excellent Introduction,[1] the Liturgical Commission set out their understanding of the needs of parents and a theological underpinning of the resource liturgy provided. Given the distinctive needs of the liturgy, it concludes with guidance that 'Words only are provided: they need to be filled out with silence, touch, actions and gestures'.

Roman Catholic liturgy

Within the Roman Catholic liturgy for perinatal death, there is less diversity. *Codex Juris Canonici* states that children whose parents had intended to have them baptised but who died before baptism, may be allowed Church funeral rites by the local ordinary.[2]

In Ireland, the 1991 Order of Christian Funerals, approved by the Irish Bishops' Conference, is used. The revised Rite of Funerals (Rome, 1969, no. 82), makes specific provision for the funeral of stillborn babies. In the funeral Mass for a child who has died before baptism, it states: 'Comfort them with the knowledge that the child for whom they grieve is entrusted now to your loving keeping'.[3]

The American liturgy for the Roman Catholic tradition is set out in the *American Order of Christian Funerals* (1989).[4] Separate readings are provided in the rite 'Funerals for Children who Died before Baptism' and alternate prayers are provided in the rite 'Vigil for a Deceased Child'. Another interesting and most appropriate change coming from the USA is found within the *Book of Blessings* (1989), which includes 'Order for the Blessing of Parents after a Miscarriage'. In the Introduction it states: 'In times of death and grief the Christian turns to the Lord for consolation and strength. This is especially true when a child dies before birth'.[5]

Methodist liturgy
The Methodist Worship Book (1999) has a specific service entitled
'A Funeral Service for a Stillborn Baby'. Its format is quite
flexible and it may be adapted as a resource following either
miscarriage or neo-natal death. From research undertaken with
bereaved families, the draft version of this service was seen as
the most helpful and pastorally appropriate.

Presbyterian liturgy
Within the Reformed Tradition, the Church of Scotland has
prepared a thorough liturgy entitled 'Funeral Service for a
Stillbirth Child' from the *Book of Common Order* (1994). The Preface
sets out the purpose of the liturgy and acknowledges the possible
feelings of emptiness, of being lost and not understanding the loss.
The Preface also sets out an excellent standard of liturgy based
upon Scripture, along with very appropriate prayers.

What seems present in this liturgy, and also in the United
Reformed Church leaflet 'When a Baby Dies', is that prominence
is given to the feelings of the parents in affirming and comforting
words. There is no discussion of whether a miscarried or stillborn
baby is a human being or not. The word 'baby' is used throughout
the liturgy and the leaflet. The view that the baby is unique is also
prominent.

Jewish liturgy
Jewish religious tradition expresses the view that a baby dying
before birth passes to the next world with a pure soul and will
participate in the resurrection of the dead. In the case of the
death of a baby during the first thirty days of life, the following
procedures take place: A post-mortem should be avoided, if
possible. Referral to a rabbi should be sought if guidance is
required. In this tradition, burial is obligatory. At the burial
service there is no obligation of the *Keriah* (the tearing of one's
clothes). Also, it is not required to have a *Minyan* (ten men)
praying at the service, as the traditional funeral prayer, the

Kaddish, is not obligatory. Naming of the baby is important, and for a boy this should be done at the time of the burial preparations. For a girl, the name should be given prior to the commencement of the burial. *Shiva* (the formal mourning practice) is not observed if the baby has lived for less than thirty days.

Islamic liturgy

Within the Islamic community, if death is less than 120 days following conception, there are no funeral prayers or liturgy and the foetus is buried. If the death of the baby occurs more than 120 days after conception, then there is a full adult funeral followed by a burial. Within this community the tradition holds that children who die and have not yet reached puberty go straight to heaven.

Other liturgies

Beyond the official liturgists of the institutional Church, other groups have produced resources for the bereaved. Sr Lamb produced a variety of liturgies in the SHARE manual *Bittersweet...hellogoodbye* (1989). This is an excellent source of material, going beyond the traditional formats of Church liturgy. Poetry, prose and purpose-written funeral services from many Christian and Jewish sources are included.

The various support groups often produce their own liturgies. Wretmark (1993) notes that it seems as if there is a dividing line between rituals that are created by those who have a close experience of dealing with loss and grief, and those that are products from the writing desk.[6] Support groups have been seen as more responsive to the needs of parents, creating appropriate liturgies quickly. In some cases the Church has been less than responsive to the needs of bereaved parents in the area of appropriate liturgy.

Walter (1990), writing on this area, notes how the support groups have moved on in meeting the needs of bereaved parents. In an age where funerals are seen very much within the sole domain of the funeral director and other professionals, it has been noted that bereaved parents are insisting on, and getting, what they want.

Wretmark (1993) suggests a number of reasons for the slowness on the part of the Church. He suggests that there is a perceived risk of minimising the necessity of baptism – whereby a naming liturgy may replace baptism. Also, there may be a fear that parents might wish to apply these liturgies for stillbirth, to situations of miscarriage. This would mean the Church would have to re-evaluate its view of personhood.

Memorial services

As in all areas of grief care, memorial services are a central part of what is available to bereaved parents. Annual remembrance services, especially at Christmas time, have been a regular feature in the life of the various support groups. ISANDS (Irish Stillbirth & Neonatal Death Society) and MAI (Miscarriage Association of Ireland) hold services at Christmas and at other times at the Holy Angels' Plot in Glasnevin. The content of these liturgies is excellent. For many families attending, such rituals become a central part of their Christmas, even many years after the death of their baby.

These memorial services differ from rituals performed close to the death of a baby, which are much more private in nature. In the memorial service, the themes are of remembrance, thanksgiving and also a balance between stressing the uniqueness of the experience and what parents have in common with other bereaved parents. These services allow those bereaved many years previously to acknowledge their baby, something that was denied at the time.

Preparing the liturgy/service: what is helpful?

By nature, the numbers attending such funeral services tend to be very small and therefore there is a great intimacy. The theological emphasis that underpins such a service is the belief that God is intimately involved in and through the pain of the grief. In such an atmosphere 'The words and actions of Jesus in welcoming and receiving young infants are very significant'.[7] It should always be remembered that the ownership of the service lies with the family and not the clergy or the funeral director. In helping families to prepare a liturgy for their baby, it must be kept in mind that a funeral is unrepeatable and therefore must be planned and designed with appropriate care and time. The following are offered for consideration in the preparation of such services with bereaved families:

- Involve the family, covering the generations of grandparents, parents and siblings.
- Encourage and facilitate the family in making their own decisions. Allow time for the various options to be considered.
- Where possible, the service should be timed so that the mother may attend. If this is not possible, consider the option of a liturgy with the mother in hospital. The funeral could be delayed in order to allow the mother to attend.
- The setting of the funeral should be intimate and comfortable – a church, family home or within the hospital setting.
- In some cases it may be appropriate to have an intimate family service, followed by a more public service. Hospital staff may well have a very helpful role in the service.
- Names are very important and should be referred to: the baby, parents, grandparents and siblings.

- The family are central to the service, in its format and involvement. Therefore encouragement should be given for prayers, prose and poetry written by family members themselves.
- The family will value the production of an Order of Service, unique to the baby, with a Certificate of Naming. Personalised liturgies are very appropriate.
- Good liturgy does not need too much explanation.
- Symbols can be a great resource, but do not overdo it.

In this chapter the importance of appropriate and sensitive ritual was explored. Such responses go beyond the traditional confines of the Church. However, for those bereaved within the Church, there continues to be a controversy about baptism – the central rite of initiation. In the following chapter the sacrament of baptism will be explored. Consideration will be given to its two-fold role. First, baptism is seen in terms of incorporation into the Christian community, and second, it is traditionally seen as the ritual through which a baby is named.

Notes:

1. *A Prayer Book of Australia* (1995), p.753.
2. Canon 1183 (2).
3. *Order of Christian Funerals* (Veritas Publications, Dublin, 1991), p.140.
4. *Order of Christian Funerals* (The Liturgical Press, Minnesota, 1989).
5. *Book of Blessings* (The Liturgical Press, Minnesota, 1989), p.86.
6. Wretmark, A.A., *Perinatal Death as a Pastoral Problem* (Almqvist & Wiksell International, Stockholm, 1993), p.273.
7. *A Prayer Book for Australia*, p.753.

8
Can Our Baby be Baptised?

Baptism is a central rite of the Christian Church and such rites have the ability to give value and meaning. Of course, such rites cannot be separated from the belief system that underpins them. The ritual of baptism, therefore, not only gives a child a name, but also marks its entry into the Christian community as a full member.

Baptism, especially in the loss of stillbirth, can be a major issue and its absence a source of anger for bereaved parents. Parents' spirituality influences, for better or worse, their emotional, mental and physical responses to bereavement. If parents hold a view that life commences at the moment of conception, and then experience the death *in utero* of their baby, this belief may influence the nature of their grief.

All families should be offered spiritual support, and for some parents baptism, by its very nature, is often seen as a central and crucial response of the Church. In personal research undertaken, some parents spoke of believing that their rights and those of their baby were being denied by the absence of baptism.

Clergy who baptise a stillborn child probably do so because they believe that the pastoral needs override Church doctrine in a crisis situation. This may occur even though the clergy in question may agree with the understanding that sacraments are for the living. In a number of individual interviews with clergy, this seemed the commonly held view in the cases of those clergy who had baptised stillborn babies during their ministry.

Church law on baptism

Church tradition has held that baptism is appropriate for those who are living. In terms of Canon Law within the Churches of the Anglican Communion, there are no rubrics or directions that state that a stillborn baby cannot be baptised. However, in the view of some canon lawyers, this apparent silence in Anglican Canon Law does not imply any agreement with the practice of baptism of stillborn babies. In Blunt (1913),[1] based upon the Council of Nismes (1284), it is stated that 'infants are to be actually born before they are baptised'. At the present time, many would question Blunt's view, given the change in understanding about the beginning and ending of life.

While baptism, in most traditions, is not deemed to be appropriate in the case of a stillborn baby, there seems to be a trend, from individual interviews conducted, of baptism being administered when requested. In a survey of fourteen United Kingdom hospital chaplains,[2] all would be willing to baptise a stillborn baby, subject to the parents' explicit request. In addition, all those interviewed stated that it would be a prerequisite that an appropriate and full explanation of the nature of baptism be given, so that baptism is not seen in terms of superstition and quasi-magical rite. Many chaplains stated that when such an explanation was given, a considerable number of parents would request a service of blessing and naming, rather than baptism.

Within Roman Catholic Canon Law the position on the sacrament is much clearer. The Sacred Congregation for the Doctrine of the Faith (CDF, 1980b) states that 'As for infants who have died without baptism, the Church can do nothing but commend them to the mercy of God, as in fact she does in the funeral rite designed for them'. This view has been seen as tempered by a comment from the Catechism (1261) which states that Jesus' tenderness toward children caused him to say: 'Let the children come to me, do not hinder them' (Mark 10:14). This allows us to hope that there is a way of salvation for children who have died without baptism. Within Roman Catholic baptismal liturgy one can note a distinction between those who are baptised and those who are not. The liturgy states that it can ensure that a baptised child is with God, whereas those without baptism are entrusted to God. Karl Rahner wrote about 'Baptism by desire', which speaks of the parents who would have wished to have their child baptised and therefore *de facto* such a infant is understood as baptised.

In 1983 the Methodist Church (UK) made a statement on the pastoral aspects of stillbirth. Within the statement the possibility of baptism is not ruled out. It acknowledges that baptism is not primarily a naming ceremony. As a tradition, it holds the view that baptism is not necessary for the salvation of the stillborn child and such baptisms are not regarded as wrong. Where bereaved parents make a request for baptism, the document suggests that if baptism seems to reassure the parents of God's favour towards the child, then the Church should support the parents' request. The United Methodist Church in America states that its understanding is that a stillborn child does not need to be baptised, for such a child is received into the love and presence of God 'because the Spirit worked in that child to bestow saving grace'.

The booklet *Miscarriage, Stillbirth and Neonatal Death* produced by the United Reformed Church (UK) states that 'The Baptism of a stillborn baby is occasionally requested by parents. Chaplains whose theological inclinations may be to refuse such a request should display much understanding'.[3] The Church of Scotland Panel on Doctrine has expressed the view that baptism is not appropriate in such situations.

Limbo and Original Sin

To gain further insights into why baptism is requested it is important to view two central theological concepts. The doctrine of original sin as expounded by St Augustine has been viewed by Hick as 'at its most extreme over emphasis as a catastrophic, damning and communicated fall from created perfection'.[4] Augustine's understanding of original sin is that all the descendants of Adam share in the guilt of that first sin in the Garden of Eden. All evil is the result of human sin and from birth all members of the human race have inherited this tendency to sin. Therefore, all humans are deserving of God's punishment and without God's grace there is no escape.

During the fourth century, the notion of the perfection of the Garden of Eden and the extent of the fall from grace grew. Augustine himself faced the challenge of Pelagius, a British monk, who held the view that human will was actually uncorrupted and, therefore, there was much less emphasis upon the need for grace to heal sin. Pelagius believed that infant baptism was not about forgiveness of sins, whereas to Augustine, baptism was very much concerned with the forgiveness of sins. To Augustine, all, including infants, are fundamentally guilty. He based his views upon the writings of St Paul (Romans 5:12-21) and his own interpretation of the first three chapters of Genesis – a view that many would challenge today.

Augustine had the view that baptism was necessary to cleanse original sin, and this led to profound problems with regard to what happened to babies who died unbaptised. The General Council of Florence (1442) declared the necessity of the baptism of infants as the only remedy for the salvation of infants. Limbo became the refuge of those who were not baptised. Thomas Aquinas held that in 'limbo' infants were merely deprived forever of the beatific vision of God.

In research undertaken with families, the issue of limbo came up a number of times, usually by parents bereaved over twenty-five years or more. In theological usage the name is applied to (a) the temporary place or state of the souls of the just who, although purified from sin, were excluded from the beatific vision until Christ's triumphant ascension into heaven (the *limbus patrum*); or (b) the permanent place or state of those unbaptised children and others who, dying without grievous personal sin, are excluded from the beatific vision on account of original sin alone (the *limbus infantium* or *puerorum*).

Linked to this was the idea that various categories of people, considered 'undesirable', were denied Christian burials, and these included pagans and excommunicates. It was believed that if one did not associate with them in life, then certainly one would not after death. Unbaptised infants fell into this 'undesirable' group and were not buried in consecrated ground.

Walsh (1994) quoting in a commentary on the Roman Catholic Catechism states: 'The Church does not endorse the tradition (which was never a defined dogma) that babies who die without the rebirth of baptism go not to a heaven, but to a state of purely natural happiness called limbo'.[5] It needs to be acknowledged that it is not easy to reverse such a popular understanding by increased clarity in theological statements. In the Vatican II Decree on the Church in the World, there has been the suggestion that the unbaptised infant shares in Christ's death and resurrection 'in a manner known only to God'.[6]

Coming from a more reformed tradition, Nash (1999)[7] takes the view that infants are incapable of moral good or evil and, therefore, he argues that infants cannot be judged. Thus, such infants are 'elect, redeemed, regenerate and glorified'. He offers the view based upon his reading of scripture that all children who die in infancy, baptised or not, are saved.

Nature of request for baptism

Having explored earlier the nature of ritual, it would be useful to tease out what is being expressed when parents request baptism for their dead baby. [8] First of all, however, it is essential to acknowledge the whole area of the personal feelings of the celebrant of the sacrament. Peter Speck, a noted hospital chaplain, in a paper delivered at the College of Health Care Chaplains Conference on the subject of Personhood (1999), stated with regard to baptism: 'Whatever the status of the foetus in law or medically at various stages we may (pastorally) attribute personhood to that foetus on the basis of our own value system or that of the couple to whom we are ministering. If our value system is different to that of the couple, is it right to impose our standard onto them or collude with what we perceive as unhelpful?' Speck continues by advocating that we must understand something of the story of the family and their understanding of God or we may end up reinforcing unhelpful views of God and prayer.

The request from some parents for baptism may be connected to a feeling that without baptism God will not accept their baby. Deep within our communal psyche, according to Hamilton, Baptism is viewed in some sense as a 'rescue, that nothing else can declare that this helpless babe ... is safe in everlasting arms'.[9] Within many families there are accounts of parents or grandparents baptising their stillborn child in response to this concern. For some parents, there is a real need for a ritual to mark what has happened, and baptism is the only ritual with which they are familiar and know to ask for. There is also the need to place their loved child into the hands of God, through a commendation. There is the need to name their child. There may also be the need to 'do something for their baby'.

Ritual is about giving expression to a reality. The use of ritual is a tangible way of marking and acknowledging the reality of the birth/death of a baby. Baptism, therefore, may be seen as a way of acknowledging the reality of the baby and the reality of the loss at the death of the baby. For some parents, perhaps unconsciously, there is still the fear (however unfounded) that unbaptised babies will be refused burial in consecrated ground.

Ramshaw (1987) argues that the Church has to develop clearer norms for the use of baptism. She explores the possibility of a 'better' ritual response to parents' needs, which would also be characterised by ritual honesty. She lists three main needs to consider:

1. That others recognise the reality of the child's existence and the parents' grief.
2. Commending the child to God.
3. Saying goodbye, and in that process beginning to let go of the hopes and dreams that were invested in anticipation of the birth of the child.

Ramshaw suggests a ritual that would include naming a child, not just in passing, but as a special act in the ritual. Included would be prayers of commendation to God's arms, as well as a special blessing for the baby, which would link in with what takes place in baptism. Also included would be prayers that acknowledge the feelings of anger, grief and questioning. Ramshaw suggests that when a chaplain receives a request for baptism of a stillborn baby, rather than saying 'No, I can't do that', a more appropriate response would be: 'We have, if you wish, a special service, with prayers for your baby'.

Stoneking, quoted in Lamb (1989), wrote on the inner turmoil as he approached parents who had requested that he baptise their stillborn baby. He wondered how he could maintain his theological integrity and yet respond to the pastoral crisis of these parents. As he awaited the birth of the baby he realised, 'Before they [the parents] would be able to say goodbye, they had to have a way to say hello'.[10] The naming means that the child is a real person and baptism is the moment in which the community of faith says welcome. 'The mother spent the only time she would ever have with her child in silence and worship'. Stoneking then spoke of God's love and the significance of the child, took the baby in his arms, and the baptism then took place.

Lamb, a religious Roman Catholic sister, was crucially involved in SHARE's book, *Bittersweet...hellogoodbye* (1989). She holds the view that the pastoral perspective is the most important issue and, therefore, for her, 'practice influences theology and theology follows practice'.

Janet Peterman (1987),[11] a Lutheran pastor, stated that baptism of stillborn babies is inappropriate because it denies God's ability to be merciful. She also expresses the concern that such a baptism takes the sacrament out of its biblical context of repentance and faith. She acknowledges that the Church needs to formulate appropriate ritual which will affirm, in the case of pregnancy loss, what is affirmed in baptism:

- The child's uniqueness before God.
- The child's belonging to the community of faith.
- The Church's recognition that the death of the child is a real loss.
- The support of the Christian community for the parents.

Thomas Moe (1997) suggests another approach whereby the controversial use of baptism/dedication can be minimised by placing the choice in the hands of the parents.[12]

Whatever theological views are held, it is imperative to provide appropriate and sensitive liturgy. In addition, there should be both clarity and simplicity of explanation of the reasons why baptism is deemed not to be the appropriate response.

Naming process

Research from many quarters points out that the naming of a baby is very important and is much more than an administrative procedure. DeFrain (1986) notes that 90 per cent of the parents included in his study had named their child. Such naming helped to show others that the infant really existed and was important. For those with any connection to the Church, baptism is viewed as the way in which we officially receive our name. The importance of a ritual for this significant rite of passage is clear.

Interestingly, there is little reference in the medical or nursing literature to baptism. Many authors – Klaus & Kennell (1976), Lewis & Page (1978) – focus upon the importance of the naming of a baby. Some of the same authors seem to stress the importance of the funeral and the presence of parents at it. It may be that those writing on the subject believe that baptism is a religious event as opposed to a funeral.

Traditionally, baptism is seen as an offering to God and a welcoming into the Church of a child or adult who is living. Walter (1990) quotes an Anglican priest whose daughter died shortly after birth. 'In practice, many chaplains have reached different conclusions ... Parents need to be sensitively aware that baptism is not a pre-condition for a child's acceptance by God. Chaplains, on the other hand, need to recognise the therapeutic value of baptism or service of blessing, as a means of affirming the child as a real person, loved by his or her parents and loved and valued by God'.[13]

This chapter sets out the need for clarity in understanding and explanation of what baptism is about. The greatest advocate for bereaved parents has often been the various support groups. In the next chapter the importance of these groups will be acknowledged. A brief history of some of the main support groups is included, as it gives a flavour of the times when parents needed to come together to support each other in the face of their common losses.

Notes:

1.   Blunt, J.H., *The Book of Canon Law* (1913).
2.   Ten Anglican and four Free-Church chaplains.
3.   *Miscarriage, Stillbirth, Neonatal Death*. A paper on pastoral care for ministers and hospital chaplains. Produced by the Ministry of Healing Committee, United Reformed Church, London.
4.   Hick, J., *Evil and the God of Love*, p.207.
5.   Walsh, M., *Commentary on the Catechism of the Catholic Church* (Cassell, London, 1994), p.249.
6.   *Gaudium et spes*, 22.
7.   Nash, R., *When a Baby Dies* (Zondervan Publishing House, Grand Rapids, 1999).
8.   Further reflections in Pierce, B., 'Baptism and Stillbirth: Theological Nonsense or Pastoral Necessity' in *Search: A Church of Ireland Journal*, Vol. 24, No.2, Winter 2001.
9.   Hamilton, D., 'When birth and death come together: the right rite?' in *Scottish Journal of Health Care Chaplaincy*, Vol. 2, No. 2, p.16.
10.   Lamb, J.M., *Bittersweet...hellogoodbye*, 2nd edn (SHARE, Illinois, 1989), p.10.
11.   Peterman, J.S., 'A pastoral and theological response to losses in pregnancy' in *The Christian Century*, Sept. 9-16, 1987.
12.   Moe, T., *Pastoral Care in Pregnancy Loss* (Haworth Press, New York, 1997), p.116.
13.   Walter, A., *Funerals and How to Improve Them* (Hodder & Stoughton, London, 1990), p.277.

9

Those Who Share the Journey – Support Groups

Grief by nature is not just an individual experience but also a communal experience. The presence and commitment of the support group has been integral in both the care of bereaved parents and in the changing attitudes on the nature of perinatal death. Research has shown the great importance and benefit of support groups to bereaved parents. Leon (1990) suggested that self-help groups were the greatest source of social support and understanding for bereaved parents. He suggested that these groups affirmed that the grief being experienced by the bereaved was normal. He also pointed out that groups provide safe places where all the emotions can be freely expressed.[1]

Many of the key writers already mentioned in this work support this view. Research through (bereaved) focus groups, following miscarriage or stillbirth, carried out for the purpose of this book, clearly showed how those involved in the support groups had been greatly helped. Many bereaved parents find that support groups are essential resources following the death of their baby. Other parents work through their grief without connecting into the support group.

Support groups offer:[2]

- A sense of community and belonging and the opportunity to be with people who are prepared to journey the extra mile with bereaved parents.
- Empathy and not just sympathy; involvement with those who have been there themselves.
- Time to tell the story as often as necessary. Bereaved parents require enormous amounts of time, support and presence, which support groups can provide.
- Ownership of the group and all those present. The bereaved can give and receive help.
- A forum where isolation following the loss can be addressed.
- A forum where feelings expressed can be seen as normal and natural.
- A safe refuge, especially for men, to share their emotional state.
- Information, reassurance and hope.
- Availability of help, often on a twenty-four-hour basis.
- The company of fellow sufferers who have made the journey and who can be a real source of hope.
- A channel of communication on behalf of parents to hospital, clergy, government, etc.
- The possibility of educating the public about the needs of bereaved parents.

It is important to differentiate between what is therapy and what occurs within a support/self-help group. Skinner Cook & Dworkin (1992) set out the following table, which helps to differentiate between self-help groups on the one hand, and therapy on the other:[3]

	Self-Help	**Therapy**
Purpose	Mutual support	Support and professional help with complicated grief
Size	Unlimited	Maximum 8–10
Leadership	Members	Trained professional(s)
Regular attendance	Not required	Required
Active participation	Not required	Required
Duration	Open-ended	Often fixed time limit
Meetings	Often once a month	Usually once a week
Cost	None	Often substantial

In a support group for bereaved parents, those attending are searching for others who both speak and understand their language of loss. Many parents feel that they are isolated and that after a while people no longer want to hear their story. Parents need to be able to speak whenever necessary and to be heard and understood. A venue that is non-judgemental and where expressing the full gambit of grief emotions is acceptable, can help parents greatly. Such an environment helps fathers especially, who are often conditioned not to express emotions or to grieve openly with their peers. Through the support-group dynamic, sharing one's grief with others who are willing to listen and are able to understand, relieves isolation. A community is fostered in the sharing, parents learn that they are not 'going crazy' and tangible approaches to problem-solving can be raised and shared within a group setting. In such a group there is no recourse to the phrase 'Get yourself together'.

The role of these groups is essential given that bereaved parents may have no other structured environment in which to share their story. Self-help groups often provide help at the different stages of the grief journey. The death of a baby often leads to feelings of either being excluded or not wanting to be involved with the activities of childbearing friends and siblings. A bereaved couple may cope with increased isolation but also have feelings of exclusion from community and families.

Woods & Woods (1997) highlight the role of support groups for bereaved parents for a subsequent pregnancy. Support groups can help parents to move towards the new baby while learning to live with their loss. Support groups can help parents to understand and in turn to use their past experiences to relate to the pregnancy.

A number of those involved in a support group may stay beyond what is a standard cycle of involvement and become facilitators, even though they have journeyed on in their own grief resolution. I sense that many parents who remain involved, beyond their grief resolution, do so in order to share their experiences, and to put back into the group something in return for all they received in their time of need.

Support groups and the changing attitudes in society

Alexander (1993) noted that SANDS (Stillbirth and Neonatal Death Society) has been very active in persuading health authorities and health professionals to recognise the need for parents to have an opportunity to grieve.[4] The support groups have been very active in making a case for changes in practice in the various pastoral and medical responses. In the Preface to The Church of England 1988 liturgy and also Common Worship 2000, acknowledgement is given to the influence of support groups. Within Ireland, ISANDS (Irish Stillbirth and Neonatal Death Society) was crucial in introducing open-ended registration in the new Stillbirth Registration Act 1994. In addition to lobbying Government agencies, the support groups have also become involved in education programmes designed to both dispel various myths and to help change attitudes.

Support groups have been central in the campaign for more appropriate and pastorally sensitive liturgy. Ramshaw (1988) noted how in the eighties an increasing feature had been the growth in memorial services and funerals for stillborn babies and also miscarried foetuses. Interestingly, the impetus came not from the institutional Church but from parents themselves, operating often within the context of a support group.

A brief history of the support groups

SANDS – Stillbirth and Neonatal Death Society
The Stillbirth Association (UK) had its origins in three years of meetings, discussions, letters and article writing and was founded in the late 1970s by Hazelanne Lewis, a psychiatric social worker and bereaved parent. It was registered as a charity in 1981, with fifty local groups already established on a national basis. Programmes presented by Ester Rantzen in 1982/83/84, entitled *The Lost Babies*, continued to keep the matter in the public arena and led to the registration for the first time of stillborn babies. In 1985 this body became SANDS (Stillbirth and Neonatal Death Society), with about 140 groups. Booklets were produced in 1986, and in the following two years another television programme, *From the Cradle to the Grave*, greatly increased public awareness of stillbirth.

In addition to working with parents, SANDS continues to work with and provide resources for healthcare professions. In 1991 SANDS produced the *Principles of Good Practice in Miscarriage, Stillbirth and Neonatal Death: Guidelines for Professionals*. These guidelines provide detailed guidance on the management of miscarriage, stillbirth and neonatal death for all professionals who come in contact with bereaved parents. A summary of the guidelines is included in this book.

ISANDS – Irish Stillbirth and Neonatal Death Society
ISANDS was set up in 1983 when a group of seven bereaved
mothers met in Dublin. This led to the production of a booklet
entitled *A Little Lifetime*, compiled by the founding members,
assisted by Dr Kevin Connolly. This booklet, funded by the
Department of Health, is for parents and families whose babies
have died around the time of birth. It is still distributed by
ISANDS and a subsequent revision was published in 1997.
Neonatal death was included in the second edition, as was the
subject of grief for children, grandparents and fathers. ISANDS
continues to organise the distribution of the booklet through
hospitals. One of the original aims of the group was to
introduce a Stillbirth Register, which came into law in 1994.

MAI – Miscarriage Association of Ireland
The Miscarriage Association of Ireland (MAI) has its origins in
the commitment of Stephanie Blanchford and Hillary Fraser.
Stephanie Blanchford had a miscarriage in 1986 and at that time
there was no comparable support group available in Ireland.
She joined the Miscarriage Association (UK), which was based
in Yorkshire. At the end of 1987, an article by Hillary Fraser
about a Belfast branch of the Miscarriage Association (UK)
appeared in *The Irish Times*. The author moved to Dublin and
placed an advertisement in a newspaper inviting those who had
suffered from a miscarriage to attend an open meeting. Over
forty people attended a meeting in her home. Initially set up as
a branch of the Miscarriage Association (UK), it then became
the Miscarriage Association of Ireland, which is now a
countrywide body.

SHARE
SHARE was founded in the autumn of 1977 at St John's
Hospital, Springfield, Illinois, USA. Its mission is to serve those
whose lives are touched by the tragic death of a baby through
miscarriage, stillbirth or newborn death. Its existence came

about through the insistence of one bereaved parent and the work of several members of hospital staff. Within four months, the first support group met. Since then, SHARE has become an international support group with over 130 'chapters'.

Compassionate Friends

The organisation Compassionate Friends was founded in Coventry, England in 1969 following the death of two young boys (Billy Henderson and Kenneth Lawley) in the Coventry and Warwickshire Hospital the previous spring. The assistant chaplain, Revd Simon Stephens, put both sets of bereaved parents in touch with one another. From this meeting they decided to form a self-help group and began to reach out to other newly bereaved parents in their area. The first USA 'chapter' was founded in 1972 and was incorporated in the USA as a non-profit organisation in 1978. Within the USA there are, at present, almost 600 chapters, with further chapters in Canada. The purpose of Compassionate Friends, as set out in their Mission Statement, is 'To assist families in the positive resolution of grief following the death of a child'. Their secondary purpose is 'To provide information and education about bereaved families in an effort to help their friends, employers, co-workers and interested professionals to be supportive'.

A common thread in the evolution of various support groups has been the personal experience of bereavement. Bereaved parents, usually mothers, who felt that their needs were not being met by what was available, pioneered many of the groups. In the face of some opposition or disquiet from a number of institutions, all of these small groups have grown, a sign that the service they offer is in demand. One senses from personal interviews with chaplains and healthcare staff, that these groups are fulfilling an essential need.

Notes:

1. Leon, I., *When a Baby Dies – Psychotherapy for Pregnancy and Newborn Loss* (Yale University Press, New Haven, 1990), p.58.
2. Sources: RTS & Sullender, R., *Grief and Growth. Pastoral Resources for Emotional and Spiritual Growth* (Paulist Press, New York, 1985), p.129.
3. Skinner Cook, A. & Dworkin, S., *Helping the Bereaved* (Basic Books, New York, 1992), p.97.
4. Alexander, H., *Experiences of Bereavement* (Lion Publishing, London, 1993), p.85.

10

Future Developments

This book has reviewed aspects of the past, how things evolved and the present pastoral response. Looking to the future, a number of issues remain for further consideration.

Over the last number of years, a major concern for parents has been the acknowledgement that organs have been retained following post-mortem. Many parents have been traumatised on learning that certain organs were removed following post-mortem without their consent or knowledge. Issues around consent and standardised procedures have been raised following inquiries into hospitals in Liverpool, at Alder Hey, and also in Bristol. Within the Irish healthcare service, organ retention is a major concern and at the time of writing the Dunne Inquiry is about to proceed.

For some parents there has been a fresh encounter with their previous grief, which has been very painful. Major emotions have been raised about trust in the healthcare services. Some parents commented that it is just another example of a paternalistic attitude that has not gone away. The Church and other caring groups have had to explore how best to meet the needs of parents with regard to what will happen to the organs that have been retained. Many parents have made the decision to leave the responsibility for the reverent disposal to the hospital. Other parents have requested a return of their child's organs so that they can be buried with the child. In research undertaken, prior to the organ retention issue becoming public, it was clear that many parents believed in the importance of the resurrection of the body. Parents spoke of meeting their babies in heaven but wondered what age their baby would be. This was a view expressed by parents who said that they themselves had little connection with the Church. If this is the case, then one can understand the anger and frustration parents have experienced on learning that organs were retained without permission.

The trauma for some parents has been compounded when faced with suggestions that such rituals are both unnecessary and bizarre. One parent commented that the language they heard when they spoke of wanting to bury the retained organ with their baby was 'just like you would have heard twenty-five years ago when you asked to be at the funeral of your baby'.

With regard to a burial or cremation of the retained organ, a personal view is that it is important to express to parents that this is a completion of what has already happened at the earlier burial rather than a second funeral. The liturgy provided for this service needs to be both appropriate and specific to the family's situation and spiritual needs. As in all liturgies with bereaved parents, considerable time must be spent in the planning of what is to happen.

Serious consideration has been, and is still being given, to how consent is sought for a post-mortem. For certain procedures, in order to identify a possible cause of death, it is necessary to remove an organ for a period of time. Some parents have requested that the funeral be delayed until the organ is returned, and this may run into months. The importance of adequate time, clarity of understanding and language is crucial in such cases. Ongoing protocols and guidelines are in the process of completion by various health authorities.

Other issues that need to be addressed, in the views of bereaved parents, centre upon early miscarriage and how such loss is acknowledged. Issues about the lack of appropriate liturgy or ritual have already been mentioned. Parents have spoken of concerns that multiple miscarriages are deemed a major problem only after three consecutive miscarriages. With the enthusiasm used by the support groups to set up the Stillbirth Register, perhaps similar energy may be expended in pressing for greater recognition of early miscarriages.

Baptism will continue to be a real issue for some parents. What will help will be the availability of appropriate naming services. Clergy need to realise that saying a direct no to the request for baptism, with no explanation, may be of little comfort to parents.

Within the changing nature of Irish society and its increasingly cosmopolitan flavour, there is a need to be aware that certain cultures may not be comfortable with what is considered current good practice. Certain cultures would be very upset with photographs of their baby being taken. There is ongoing need to be culturally and religiously sensitive to the needs of each individual case. Making assumptions can lead to many problems and unintended hurt.

In conclusion, changes have come about in the various pastoral responses to miscarriage and stillbirth because of new insights into the value ascribed to the grief of parents. In the years to come, a similar approach of being open to change and being sensitive to the needs of parents in their grief, is essential and obligatory on all those who care.

11
Liturgies Following Miscarriage or Stillbirth

Preface to Liturgy section
The following prayers and liturgies come from a variety of traditions and are intended for various pastoral situations. The inclusion of any prayer does not imply the author's preference or approval for its content or theological stance. Flexibility and adaptability are important criteria in the drawing up of appropriate liturgy. The following, I hope, will provide a useful framework for preparing a service with family members.

Liturgy 1: Blessing of a Child

Introduction:

Chaplain: We begin by reminding ourselves that wherever we are, in Church, at home, out in the fresh air, or here in hospital, we are always in God's presence.

He has been with us in the past, he will be with us in the future, and he is with us now, to hear us, to support us and to comfort us.

So we meet, as always ✠ in the Name of the Father, and of the Son, and of the Holy Spirit. **Amen.**

All: **Almighty God, we thank you for your presence now. We thank you that you are here with us to support and comfort us, and we thank you that in your Name a blessing for this child can take place. Be with us in this special act of dedication; be with us now and always. Amen.**

Chaplain: I name this child, and sign him/her with the sign of the cross, the badge that all Christians wear, ✠ in the Name of the Father, and of the Son, and of the Holy Spirit. **Amen.**

Jesus taught us a family prayer, which in confidence we pray together:

All: **Our Father**

Chaplain: The Blessing of God almighty, Father, Son and Holy Spirit, be with you, and those whom you love, now and always. **Amen.**

(Source: Revd Philip Carrington, South Tees Hospital Trust, Middlesbrough.)

Liturgy 2: Blessing of a Stillborn Baby

(Name), as your body is marked with the cross, so may your soul be blessed by the Holy Spirit now and for all eternity.

Almighty God, who gave joy to this child's parents in the knowledge that he/she had been conceived, we commend them now to your love in their great sadness.

May they be supported by the love of family and friends, and consoled in the knowledge that in your care they and their child are forever united. **Amen.**

Lord, bless the brothers and sisters of (*this child/name*) in their special sadness.

May they remember his/her love as a member with them of the family, and cherish all memories that they have since they first knew their brother/sister to be.

Remember, Lord, the soul of this child, who has gone before us with the sign of faith, and who rests in the sleep of death.

To him/her, Lord, and all who rest in Christ, grant a place of refreshment, light and peace in the love of your Risen Son, Jesus Christ. **Amen.**

May almighty God, Father, Son and Holy Spirit, bless you all, now and forever. **Amen.**

(Source: Revd Hugh Sargent, Chaplaincy Dept., Southampton General Hospital.)

Liturgy 3: A Service for all Faiths

Celebrant: Let us gather our thoughts and prayers together to celebrate the very short life of this child whom we now commemorate. We name those who shared in the joy of his/her existence and who mourn with his/her death.

We acknowledge the love that has surrounded this child and we acknowledge the disappointment and grief at the loss of him/her.

(Name of parents), you have given and shared the gift of life. May you be upheld with love as you bear the agony of separation from this child.

(Name of mother), you have carried and nurtured this life with your body and your blood. May your soul experience the gift of healing as you grieve your loss.

(Name of father), you have shared in this pregnancy with (Name of mother). You, too, have suffered a loss of hopes and dreams for this baby. May you experience healing and gain strength as you journey through this difficult time.

As people who hope in the power of love, we now acknowledge the place this child holds in our family and in our hearts. In honour of the brief time that he/she was embodied with us, I ask you what name you give your child.

The parents name their child.

Parents: We do this that we might give voice to our longing for him/her, our grief at the loss of him/her and our thoughts and prayers on his/her behalf.

O Creator, give us the grace to honour and remember our child *(Name)*. Let our love for him/her show forth in our lives. Sustain us in love and in the sacred mystery of life. May we know a sense of comfort as we go forth from this moment into our lives.

May we be blessed in our memory of *(Name)*.
May he/she never be forgotten in the circle of life.

All: **Amen.**

(Source: Betty Lynch Power, Chaplaincy Department, Mount Sinai Hospital, Toronto.)

Liturgy 4: A Service for the Family in a Home Setting

Leader: In the name of the Father and of the Son and of the Holy Spirit. **Amen.**

May Christ Jesus, who welcomed little children and laid his hands in blessing upon them, fill you with his peace and be always with you.

Family: **And also with you.**

We've brought *(Name)* home. What should have been a wonderful occasion has turned to heartbreak. Yes, *(Name)* is home. For it was here that he/she lived for those very short nine months.

It was here with *(Name)* and *(Name)*, his/her parents, that he/she was loved into life. And it is here that he/she will always be loved.

Life in this house revolved around him/her as plans and dreams and hope took shape. They lie shattered in broken dreams today. Hearts broken with love for him/her. Those hearts were his/her home long before he/she was ever conceived. Hearts that are his/her home and always will be.

'See! I will not forget you... I have carved you in the palm of my hand.' (Isaiah 49:16)

(Name), you are carved in your parents' hearts.
In our pain and grief, we find some consolation in God's word –

'Before I formed you in the womb, I knew you.'
(Jeremiah 1:5)

(Name) is fully known and enfolded in the personal love of God, in the palm of whose hand we are all held. *(Name)* has gone to his/her true home and lives in the palm of God's hand. This doesn't take the pain away, but in time it will take some of the sting of the pain that we all feel now.

Leader: Let us pray.
Tender and loving God, be with us as we gather in sadness to welcome *(Name)* to the home where the love of *(Father)* and *(Mother)* gave him/her life. We thank you for the gift of life, however so brief, and we place *(Name)* safely in your care.
We make our prayer through Jesus Christ our Lord.

Family: **Amen.**

Leader: A reading from the holy Gospel according to St Mark (4:30-32).

He also said, 'With what can we compare the kingdom of God, or what parable will we use for it? It is like a mustard seed, which, when sown upon the ground, is the smallest of all the seeds on earth; yet when it is sown it grows up and becomes the greatest of all shrubs, and puts forth large branches, so that the birds of the air can make their home in its shade.'

Family: **Praise to you, Lord Jesus Christ.**

Leader: Loving God, we believe that *(Name)* is at home with you. We trust in your promise to keep all of us in mind. In these painful moments, it is love that makes us cry and it is your healing hand that wipes away our tears. Keep us strong in your love. We ask this through Christ, our Lord.

Family: **Amen.**

Leader: Together we pray for strength, for acceptance, for the coming of God's Kingdom, which is our true home, using the very prayer that Jesus himself has given us.

Family: **Our Father...**

Concluding Prayer

Leader: O Lord, whose ways are beyond our understanding, listen to our prayers as we struggle to understand. Grant that *(Father)* and *(Mother)* weighted down by their grief at the loss of *(Name)*, may find reassurance in your infinite goodness. We ask this through Christ our Lord.

Family: **Amen.**

Blessing

Leader: May the love of God and the peace of our Lord Jesus Christ bless and console you and gently wipe every tear from your eyes.

Family: **Amen.**

(Source: Sr Eliza Hopkins, National Maternity Hospital, Dublin 2.)

Liturgy 5: Funeral Service for a Baby

Introduction

Chaplain: Come among us, O God.
You, who cast the planets into space
And know every falling sparrow.

All: **Come God, and meet us here.**

Chaplain: Come among us, O God.
You, who bless the poor and broken
And stand by the sad and strong.

All: **Come God, and meet us here.**

Chaplain: Come among us, O God.
You, who dance in the silence
And shine in the darkness.

All: **Come God, and meet us here.**

Psalm: *Verses from Psalm 139*
You yourself created my inmost parts;
you knit me together in my mother's womb.

I will thank you because I am marvellously made;
your works are wonderful and I know it well.

My body was not hidden from you, while I
was being made in secret and woven in the
depths of the earth.

Your eyes beheld my limbs, yet unfinished in
the womb; all of them were written in your
book; they were fashioned day by day, when
as yet there was none of them.

How deep I find my thoughts, O God!
How great is the sum of them!

If I were to count them, they would be more in
number than the sand; to count them all, my
life span would need to be like yours.

Prayers: 'The Lord's Prayer'
Loving Father, you have created the world as an
expression of your love, and invited women and
men to join in your act of creation as an
expression of their love. Be with those whose child
has died. May they be close to each other, support
each other
and grow in love and understanding together.
Amen.

Period of silence and prayers

Jesus said 'Let the children come to me and do not
stop them, for the kingdom of God belongs to
them'.

Commendation of Baby
O God, as this child was cradled in the womb,
cradle him/her and hold him/her now,
that as we let him/her go, we may know that he/she
has gone from
our loving presence into yours forever.
In Jesus' name we pray. **Amen.**

Blessing
> We cannot care for you the way we wanted,
> or cradle you or listen for your cry;
> but, separated as we are by silence,
> love will not die.
>
> We cannot watch you grow into childhood
> and find a new uniqueness every day;
> but special as you would have been among us,
> you still will stay.
>
> We cannot know the pain or the potential
> which passing years would summon or reveal;
> but for that true fulfilment Jesus promised
> we hope and feel.
>
> So through the mess of anger, grief and tiredness,
> through tensions which are not yet reconciled,
> we give to God the worship of our sorrow
> and our dear child.
>
> Lord, in your arms which cradle all creation
> we rest and place our baby beyond death,
> believing that he/she now, alive in heaven,
> breathes with your breath.

(This service incorporates material from the Iona Community.
Source: Revd Jane Richards, Pastoral Care Team, Southampton
General Hospital.)

Liturgy 6: Memorial Service to Remember Precious Babies

(An opportunity for those who have experienced the loss of a
baby, however small, to come together.)

Welcome and Introduction

Music; lighting of candles

Hymn   Fleetingly known; yet ever remembered,
              These our children, now and always;
              These whom we see not, we will forget not,
              Morning and evenings, all our days.

              Lives that touched our lives, tenderly, briefly,
              Now in the one light living always.
              Named in our hearts, now, safe from all harm,
              We will remember, all of our days.

              As we recall them, silently name them,
              Open our hearts Lord, now and always;
              Grant to us, grieving, love for the living;
              Strength for each other, all of our days.

              Safe in your peace, Lord, hold these our children,
              Grace, light and laughter, grant them each day;
              Cherish and hold them, till we may know them,
              When to your glory we find our way.

(Tune: 'Morning has broken')

Reading   You were going to be my friend
              with straight or curly hair,
              with green, brown, blue eyes,
              with ten fingers and ten toes.
              You might not have any shoes

after you were born, but you
are the pride and joy of that sad morn.

(Molly Sherman – your big sister)

Reading   Mark chapter 10: 13-16.

Reflection   Given by hospital chaplain

Act of Remembrance
(Music will be played during this time. A time of stillness,
during which flowers of remembrance of children will be
offered.)

Holding our children's names before God...

In the rising of the sun, and in its going down...
We remember them.
In the blowing of the wind, and in the chill of
winter...
We remember them.
In the opening of buds, and in the warmth of
summer...
We remember them.
In the rustling of leaves, and the beauty of
autumn...
We remember them.
In the beginning of the year, and when it ends...
We remember them.
When we are weary and in need of strength...
We remember them.
When we are lost and sick at heart...
We remember them.
When we have joys we yearn to share...
We remember them.

So long as we live they, too, shall live, for they are
part of us, as...
We remember them.

Prayers

When pain is searing,
when your heart is breaking,
hope is sinking
in a sea of grief,
then feel the spirit leading
for on your behalf he's pleading
and now hear what your father
wants to say to you...
'I love you my child.
I'll never let you go and I cry with you.
I'm there in your despair, holding you close in arms
that care.
Nothing in life or death can guard my love for you'.

When guilt condemns you, when your thoughts
oppress you,
youthful dreams have turned to bitterness.
Then see the Son whose dying on a cross for our
redeeming
and now hear what your father wants to say to you .

I am a flickering flame.
My mind is full of doubt and pain.
I find it hard even to speak your name,
but Jesus make me whole again and let me feel your
arms around me.
Let me know your love.
Show that none can part me from your love.
Lead to a future more where pain and sorrow cease
and all is light and joy in the land of peace.

Where Jesus reigns eternally
and I will feel your arms around me.
I will know your love.
Nothing there will part me from your love.

Music   'Pie Jesu'

Final Hymn

Peace is flowing like a river,
Flowing out through you and me,
Spreading out into the desert,
Setting all the captives free,
Setting all the captives free.

Love is flowing ...

Joy is flowing ...

Faith is flowing ...

Hope is flowing ...

Blessing:

Deep peace of the running wave to you.
Deep peace of the flowing air to you.
Deep peace of the quiet earth to you.
Deep peace of the shining stars to you.
Deep peace of the Son of peace to you.

(Source: Revd Helena Cermakova, Bristol Children's Hospital.)

12
Occasional Prayers, Meditations, Poems and Other Resources

Occasional prayers

- Bidding/Welcome/Gathering
- Thanksgiving for life
- Prayer of remembrance
- For the parents and family
- For the mother
- For the father
- Other prayers and rituals (Reading for a miscarried baby; prayer in time of pain; parents' prayer at farewell ritual; sign of the cross ritual)
- Prayers to use with children
- Thanksgiving for those who cared
- Commendation and farewell prayers
- Committal prayers

Bidding/welcome/gathering prayers
We gather today in the face of a terrible loss. We are overwhelmed by the mystery of life and death that we have experienced in (*Name*).
We come together as family and friends to support each other by our love and prayers.

We grieve over the ending of (*Name*)'s life so near its beginning.
Jesus loves all little children.
He died and rose again to bring them and us to the fullness of
life.
And so we celebrate God's never-ending love for us, even in the
face of death, disappointment and dashed hopes.[1]

We meet in God's loving presence to acknowledge our loss of
one so young. God knows and loves this child, whose parents (A
and B) have given her/him the name (*Name*). We ask God's
grace that in our pain we may find comfort; in our sorrow,
hope; in our questioning, understanding; and in the experience
of death, resurrection.[2]

Lord, without our consent we are born, without our consent
we live, without our consent we die, without our consent our
bodies return to the grave and our spirit goes forward to life
everlasting. We cannot always see your ways, for our minds are
overwhelmed and our eyes are too weak. Yet to comfort us and
to give us hope you lift the veil of eternity, and we are
permitted to know that the world is a corridor and we are on a
journey, that the end is perfection and the reward is peace.

For a short time you gave into our care a child whom we loved.
Our hearts would be broken if we did not know that you are
love itself, which makes good all that is lost. The tears would
never leave our eyes if we did not know that at the end you
bring all together, with mercy and tenderness, in the gathering
of life.[3]

We gather here in grief and pain. In this moment there is no
understanding, only emptiness of sorrow and loss. This little
child has died during birth (or even before he/she was born).
We are overwhelmed by the mystery of life and death that we
have experienced in him/her.

Yet we remember, in our confusion and distress, that the eternal God is here, the One whose love is seen in Jesus Christ.
On the cross, Jesus bears our pain.
Through the cross, God shares our pain.
In the Spirit, God is with us
Offering comfort, peace and love.[4]

Prayers of thanksgiving
Lord of all life, thank you for your work in creation, for nourishing life in the womb, for your love even in death. Thank you for the life of this child (*Name*), whom you gave to us and have taken to yourself. Thank you for the arms of your love, embracing both us and (*Name*) in your family.
Thank you for your presence in our sorrow, your strength as our life goes on.
Take our sadness, and fill us with your Spirit to serve you on earth, and join your saints in glory, through Jesus Christ our Lord.[5]

God of power and might, your kingdom honours the simplicity of children. Thank you for the gift of baby (*Name*), for the love and trust she/he inspired in the hearts of those to whom she/he came. Thank you for the joy she/he gave to all who knew her/him, and for the precious memories, which still abide. Accept our thanks in Jesus' name.[6]

Heavenly Father, your love for all children is strong and enduring. We were not able to know (*Name*) as we hoped. Yet you knew her/him growing in her/his mother's womb. In the midst of sadness, we thank you that (*Name*) is with you now.[7]

For the parents and family
O God, we do not understand why you would let us anticipate a birth only to be pained by death. Help us to trust your goodness and wisdom when our understanding and wisdom

fall short. We ask you this day for courage and strength, and a growing understanding of your loving presence.[8]

God our creator, from whom all life comes, comfort this family, grieving for the loss of their hoped for child. Help them to find assurance that with you nothing is wasted or incomplete, and uphold them with your love, through Jesus Christ our Saviour.[9]

For the mother

Lord Jesus, your Mother Mary stood by when you were dying. Be near to this mother (Name). Be to her a strong and loving friend. Give her healing for her hurt, and hope in place of desperation, for you alone can show us how to triumph over death.[10]

God of all mercy, you have brought your daughter (Name) safely to this day, a day when long-cherished hopes have been dashed. May she know your comfort in this time of sadness, and enjoy your protection always. Through Jesus Christ our Lord.[11]

For the father

Man of sorrows, Jesus of Nazareth, make your presence known to (Name) in his time of grief. In place of emptiness let him know your love. In place of confusion let him know your peace. In place of despair let him find hope and strength in you.
Give (Name) strength to stand by his partner, to share his deepest feelings, to follow your example of strong caring, and to receive your comfort.[12]

Other prayers and rituals

A reading for a miscarried baby

Today we come together in sorrow over the death of (Mother's Name) and (Father's Name)'s baby. Their child, created in love and eagerly wished for, has died – never to be nestled securely in their arms in their lifetime. To these parents, the pain and the disappointment is great and their loss will be carried heavily in their hearts for all their days. In the weeks and months ahead, they will miss their child terribly and will be in need of love, compassion, time and understanding from all of us.

Each life comes into this world with a mission. Sometimes the mission or purpose is clear; sometimes it is vague and shrouded in misunderstandings. In time, we will see what the baby's mission was on earth. Could it have been just to add a little flicker of love that otherwise may never have been lit? Was it to soften our hearts so that we may in turn comfort others? Could it have been to bring us closer to our God and each other?

This child's life was short, yet the death has left a huge void in all of our hearts and lives. Let us remember today and for always the tiny baby who will never see childhood or adulthood, but will remain our tiny baby forever.[13]

A prayer in time of pain (adapted)
Lord, out of your understanding and mercy reach out to us.
Hold us, comfort us, and let us know that we will laugh again from a happiness that is as profound as our grief at this moment.
It feels as though our hearts have been torn from deep inside us. The ache is more than we can bear and we are not certain if we can live with such pain.
Touch us with your tender caress and give us comfort.
We need to feel some relief, just a few moments when our minds will be still, and quiet peace will settle upon our souls.
You can do that, Lord. Give us peace and quietness.[14]

Parents' prayer at farewell ritual

O God, who has given life and beginning to our special baby, you are ever more ready than we are to pray. You know our needs before we ask, and our ignorance in asking. Give to us now your grace, that as we shrink before the mystery of death we may see the light of eternity. Speak to our hearts. Help us to love as those who have hope and who look forward to union with all we love.

We praise you for those dear to us whom we remember in our hearts before you. We praise you for the precious beginnings of our baby whom you have taken to yourself. Help us so to believe what we have not seen, that your presence may lead us through our years, and bring us at last with them into the joy of your home not made with hands, but eternal in the heavens. We pray this in, with and through Jesus, your Son. Amen.

(Alternate closing: We bring our prayer before You, our loving God. Amen.)[15]

Ritual – the Sign of the Cross

During this ritual the minister places the sign of the cross on the child and the parents may be given the opportunity, if desired, to each share in placing the sign of the cross on their child. Water is not used.

God says:

'Before I formed you in the womb I knew you.' (Jeremiah 1: 5)

And we remember that Jesus welcomed little children, took them in his arms and blessed them. (Luke 18: 15–17)

For N./all, he lived.
For N./all, he died.
Nor N./all, he rose again.
He has welcomed N./this child
into his eternal kingdom.

Therefore, as a mark of that love and grace,
we place on him/her the sign of the cross.

Let us pray:
God of compassion,
help us to believe that N./this child,
a lamb of your flock, is in your gentle care
through the grace of our Lord Jesus Christ. Amen.[16]

A prayer for use with children
Please listen, God, while we talk to you about (*Name*) who has
died. Please take care of her/him, and please take care of us
too.
Thank you for the time we had together, even though it was
very short. Thank you for Jesus, who shows us your love. He is
close to (*Name*), and he is close to us. Thank you, God.[17]

A prayer for a very young child
Gentle God, please love our baby who has come to be with you.
Mommy and Daddy said our baby was not able to live here any
more,
so (*name*) has gone to live with you.
Bless Mommy and Daddy so that they won't be so sad.
Bless me too, God, because I am very sad.
Help us all to be happy again.[18]

Thanksgiving for caregivers
God of all comfort, thank you for those who have cared in
recent days (*medical and nursing staff, those who have prayed,
friends and family, particularly...*).
Through them we have felt something of your love. We bless
you for their skill, compassion and time, and ask you to bless
and sustain them. Thank you for all they mean to us.[19]

Commendation and farewell prayers

God of all consolation, searcher of mind and heart, the faith of these parents (*Name* and *Name*) is known to you. Comfort them in the knowledge that the child for whom they grieve is entrusted now to your loving care. We ask this through Christ our Lord.[20]

Let us commend baby (*Name*) to the love of God.
Dear God, Jesus took children in his arms and blessed them.
Into your strong hands we entrust this precious baby (*Name*), a sheep of your fold, a lamb of your flock.
We believe that Jesus died and rose again to save us, and so we offer this prayer in his name.[21]

Let us commend (*Name*) to God.
Heavenly Father, we thank you for (*Name*), and commend her/him to your perfect mercy and wisdom, for in you alone we put our trust.[22]

Leader: Merciful God, your spirit intercedes for us even when we do not know how to pray. Be present among us now that we might commend (*Name*) into your loving care and, by your presence, find comfort.
Family: **Amen.**
Leader: O Child (or, *Name*), we entrust you to God who created you. May you return to the One who formed you out of the dust of the earth.
Family: **Amen.**
Leader: May this child (or, *Name*), and all the departed, through the mercy
of God, rest in peace.
Family: **Amen.**[23]

Dear God, into your almighty hands we commend this precious baby, (Name). Our hearts are full and hurting. Give us such faith that at all times and in all places we can entrust to your love those whom we hold so dear. Reassure us that our baby rests in loving arms and in the fullness of time bring healing and peace to us. Be our strength through this time of bereavement and grieving and bring us safely to times of greater peace and joy.[24]

Jesus, you drew the children close to you in this world, and because of their innoncence you hold them close to yourself in the life to come. Receive in peace the soul of this infant, (Name), for you have said, 'Of such is my kingdom in heaven'. [25]

We come to you, O God, you gave life to this precious child, (Name). We belong to you and will some day also return to be with you. We commend this child to you. Confidently trusting in your goodness and all-embracing love, we pray that you give him/her happiness for ever.[26]

Loving God, we now commend our precious little (Name) to your loving arms to caress him/her in your kindness. Touch the hearts of the parents and family, bringing healing and peace into their lives. Enlighten and strengthen their faith and bring hope to their grieving hearts.

Great God of mercy, be with each member in this time of sorrow and pain. Comfort each of us with the hope and knowledge that this infant (Name) has found a home with you and all children who have died. May he/she be welcomed into the company of the Holy Innocents who witnessed to the faith by their deaths. We come to you, our Creator, our Saviour and Redeemer.[27]

Committal prayers
Blessed be the God and Father of our Lord Jesus Christ, the
Father of mercies and God of all comfort, who comforts us in
all our affliction.
'As a mother comforts her child, so shall I myself comfort you',
says the Lord.
Like a shepherd he will tend his flock and with his arm keep
them together.

Gracious God, you have made nothing in vain and love all that
you have made.
We therefore commit (*Name*)'s body *to be cremated/to the
elements/to be buried,* earth to earth, ashes to ashes, dust to dust;
in sure and certain hope of the resurrection to eternal life,
through Jesus Christ; to whom be glory for ever and ever.[28]

Scripture resources
A central part of a funeral liturgy will be the use of Scripture.
In choosing scriptural passages it is useful to look at various
translations, conscious of differences that may help or hinder
families. The following is just a selection. The chosen text may
be incorporated as a heading in the order of service or as a
reading.

Careful consideration should be given to the appropriateness of
the readings.

Old Testament

Ecclesiastes 3:1-11	...a time to mourn ...
Isaiah 40:11	He tends his flock like a shepherd ...
Isaiah 40: 29	He gives strength to the weary ...
Isaiah 43:1-5	...I have redeemed you ...
Isaiah 49:1	Before I was born ...
Isaiah 49:16	Engraved on the palm of my hand ...
Isaiah 61:1-3	The Spirit of the Sovereign Lord ...

Jeremiah 1:5	Before you were born ...
Jeremiah 31:15	Rachel weeps for her children ...
Psalm 22:1	My God, my God, why have you forsaken me?
Psalm 23:1	The Lord is my shepherd ...
Psalm 46:1-3	God our refuge ...
Psalm 61:1-4	Hear my cry O God ...
Psalm 121:1	I lift up my eyes to the hills ...
Psalm 139:1-18	...in my mother's womb ...

New Testament

Matthew 5:1-12	Beatitudes
Matthew 11:25-30	Come to me all you who are weary ...
Matthew 19:13-15	Let the children come to me ...(Also Mark 10:13–17; Luke 18:15–17)
Mark 4:35-41	The stilling of the storm
Luke 9:46-48	Welcoming of a child
Luke 24:13-32	The road to Emmaus
John 10:11-18	I am the Good Shepherd ...
John 11:25-26	I am the resurrection and the life ...
John 14:1-6, 27	In my Father's house are many rooms ...
Romans 8:14-18	...heirs of heaven ...
Romans 8:35-39	Who shall separate us ...
Romans 14:7-9	...we belong to the Lord ...
1 Corinthians 13:4-13	...the greatest of these is love ...
2 Corinthians 1:3-5	God comforts us
Ephesians 3:14-21	...the whole family in earth and heaven is named ...
1 John 3:1-2	We are already Children of God.
Revelation 7:16-17	...every tear will be wiped away ...
Revelation 21:1-7	...there will be no death ...

Other meditations and reflections for family or worship leaders

General

Sometimes
Sometimes love is for a moment.
Sometimes love is for a lifetime.
Sometimes a moment is a lifetime.

Early miscarriage

A snowflake
A snowflake falls so gently
It has a beauty within it.
Each is unique and fragile,
Millions fall unseen,
Their beauty ignored.
They gently melt unknown to anyone.
We knew you
And we remember.

Pat Clunas

Late miscarriage
Today we come together in sorrow over the death of (*Mother's Name*) and (*Father's Name*)'s baby. Their child, created in love and eagerly awaited, has died – never to be nestled securely in their arms in their lifetime. To these parents, the pain and disappointment is great and their loss will be carried heavily in their hearts for all their days. In the weeks and months ahead, they will miss their child terribly and will be in need of love, compassion, time and understanding from all of us.

Each life comes into this world with a mission. Sometimes the mission or purpose is clear; sometimes it is vague and shrouded in misunderstandings. In time, we will see what this baby's mission was on earth. Could it have been just to add a little flicker of love that otherwise may never have been lit? Was it to soften our hearts so that we may in turn comfort others? Could it have been to bring us closer to our God and each other?

This child's life was short, yet the death has left a huge void in all of our hearts and lives. Let us remember today and for always the tiny baby who will never see childhood or adulthood, but will remain our tiny baby forever.

Susan Erling[29]

Stillbirth

We need not walk alone
They say you died at birth – how wrong they are?
For the weeks and months, wrapped in love's cocoon,
You seemed already one of us –
How we laughed and dreamed!
When you were born that day/night
With eyes gently closed against all cruelty,
Your tiny hands forged tighter family ties –
Your special warmth, a blessed radiance
That hallows all our lives.

Marion H. Youngquist (adapted)

Signposts
We had you for a little while
Growing with every scan
Together,
Allowing dormant dreams to germinate,
To permeate,
Giving birth to hope
Long before you actually arrived.
Seeing your head,
Your beating heart,
The legs which were not still,
Looking for hands
And every little signpost
On the journey into life,
Crystallised in the choosing of a name
Long before you came.
We had you for a little
And the life we mourn
Is nine months of knowing,
Nine months of growing
And many more months of hope.
We mourn the death of a dream
That had only just begun,
We mourn the loss of love,
Both the giving and the getting.
We had you in our arms
For such a short time,
Much longer in our hearts
And longer still in our dreams.

Brian Callan (adapted)

Other resources

Bittersweet...hellogoodbye. A resource in planning farewell rituals when a baby dies. Sr Jane Marie Lamb OSF (1989).
National Share Office, St Joseph Health Care Centre,
300, First Capitol Drive, St Charles, MO 63301-2893, USA.

An Empty Cradle A Full Heart. Reflections for mothers and fathers after miscarriage, stillbirth, or infant death. Christine O'Keeffe Lafser (1998).
Loyola Press, 3441 North Ashland Ave, Chicago, Illinois 60657, USA.

A Part of Ourselves. Laments for lives that ended too soon.
Edited Siobhán Parkinson (1997).
A & A Farmar, 78 Ranelagh Village, Dublin 6, Ireland.

Enduring Sharing Loving. For all those affected by the death of a child.
Edited by Marilyn Shawe (1992).
Darton, Longman and Todd (in association with the Alder Centre).

Signature of Love. A collection of poems on losing a baby.
Brian Callan (1992).
Limetree Press, 8, Limetrees Road East, Douglas, Cork, Ireland.

In terms of additional liturgical resources the following should also be considered:
A Service to Follow the Birth of a Stillborn Baby, or the Death of a Newly-born Child.
The Uniting Church of Australia (1994).

Pastoral Prayers: A Resource for Pastoral Occasions
Mowbray, London (1996).

Notes:

1. Copyright © 1995, The Anglican Church of Australia Trust Corporation. From the text of *A Prayer Book for Australia*, published under the imprint of Broughton Books. Reproduced with permission.
2. From *The Methodist Worship Book* © 1999, Trustees for Methodist Church House.
3. *A Jewish Funeral Service Book.*
4. Used with permission of the National Working Group on Worship, The Uniting Church of Australia.
5. Copyright © 1995, The Anglican Church of Australia Trust Corporation. From the text of *A Prayer Book for Australia*, published under the imprint of Broughton Books. Reproduced with permission.
6. Ibid.
7. Ibid.
8. Ibid.
9. This copyright material is taken from 'A New Zealand Prayer – He Karakia o Aoteroa' and is used with permission.
10. Copyright © 1995, The Anglican Church of Australia Trust Corporation. From the text of *A Prayer Book for Australia*, published under the imprint of Broughton Books. Reproduced with permission.
11. Ibid.
12. Ibid.
13. Reprinted with permission from *Bittersweet hello...goodbye* (SHARE, 1989) by Susan Erling.
14. Reprinted with permission from *Comfort Us Lord, Our Baby Died* (Centering Corporation).
15. Reprinted with permission from *Bittersweet...hellogoodbye* (SHARE, 1989).
16. Used with permission of the National Working Group on Worship, The Uniting Church of Australia.
17. This copyright material is taken from 'A New Zealand Prayer – He Karakia o Aoteroa' and is used with permission.
18. Reprinted with permission from *Comfort Us Lord, Our Baby Died* by Norman Hagley (Centering Corporation).
19. Copyright © 1995, The Anglican Church of Australia Trust Corporation. From the text of *A Prayer Book for Australia*, published under the imprint of Broughton Books. Reproduced with permission.

20. Copyright © 1995, The Anglican Church of Australia Trust Corporation. From the text of *A Prayer Book for Australia*, published under the imprint of Broughton Books. Reproduced with permission.
21. Ibid.
22. From *The Methodist Worship Book* © 1999 Trustees for Methodist Church House.
23. Reprinted with permission from *Bittersweet...hellogoodbye* (SHARE, Illinois, 1989) – a prayer by Revd Janet Peterman.
24. Reprinted with permission from *Bittersweet...hellogoodbye* (SHARE, 1989).
25. Ibid.
26. Ibid.
27. Ibid.
28. From *The Methodist Worship Book* © 1999, Trustees for Methodist Church House.
29. Reprinted with permission from *Bittersweet...hellogoodbye* (SHARE, 1989).

13
Principles of Good Practice for Professionals

1. The care given to parents should be responsive to their individual feelings and needs.

All those who are bereaved by the loss of a baby have experiences and feelings in common. But, however much is shared, bereavement and grief are also intensely individual, so while it is helpful if professionals recognise and understand common patterns in parents' experiences, the care and support that they give should be determined by parents' particular needs.

It is necessary:

- To avoid assumptions.
- listen and respond to each parent as an individual.
- To take account of particular circumstances, feelings and beliefs, and experiences.
- To tailor what is said and what is done to the parents/family concerned.
- Not to be judgmental.

2. Parents need information.

At every stage, parents need and should be given information that is accurate and this should be communicated clearly, sensitively and promptly.

In order that they can begin to understand and own their own experiences, parents need information:

- About what has happened, what is happening or what may happen to them.
- About practical matters, procedures and arrangements.
- About the choices that are open to them. They also need clear, factual, unbiased information so that they can make those choices.

3. Communication with parents should be clear, sensitive and honest.

It is essential that professionals are able to communicate with parents in ways that the parents find acceptable and supportive.

It is helpful if professionals are able:

- To set aside their professional authority when necessary and show a human face.
- To talk with parents on equal terms, for example, sitting not standing, and not hiding their own grief about what has happened. Important discussions should not be held while a woman is lying down, unless this clearly cannot be avoided.
- To use language that is clear, caring and easy to understand. It is important to avoid unnecessary medical jargon. This means, for example, speaking of a 'miscarriage', never of 'an abortion', and referring to the baby as 'a baby', and not as 'a foetus', no matter how small it is. Instead of talking about 'disposal' of a pre-viable baby, staff might talk about 'what will be done with the baby's body'.
- To be open and honest. Parents would rather know the truth than feel that information is being withheld from them

or misrepresented. It is particularly important not to hold discussions in parents' presence, which are not shared with them.

- To make time (and show that there is time) for lengthy and unhurried conversations when needed. Even if a conversation has to be postponed, parents will be helped if a firm promise is made to talk later.
- To recognise when a parent does or does not want to talk.

4. Parents should be treated with respect and dignity.
Parents need respect for themselves, for what they have experienced and are experiencing, and for their feelings. Their dignity is extremely important at a time when they are vulnerable. This applies equally to both parents: the father as well as the mother.

Demonstrating respect involves:

- Recognising the significance of what has happened and therefore not minimising it.
- Caring for parents in a way that does not deprive them of dignity.
- Treating and speaking about what has been lost, whether a baby, a foetus or products of conception, in a respectful way.
- Recognising the personal and private nature of grief by caring in a non-intrusive way and giving parents the privacy they need. For many parents, a hospital is an inappropriate, impersonal and public place in which to grieve.
- Enabling parents to participate in the management of their loss.

5. Parents' loss should be recognised and acknowledged, their experiences and feelings validated.
Parents need others to recognise and acknowledge their loss as part of the difficult process of accepting what has happened. This need, like grief itself, continues over a long period of time.

The expression of sympathy is one important and very simple form of acknowledgement. Parents may also need confirmation of the reality of their experience and reassurance about their responses to it. They may need support to do things that will make their experiences real for them and create memories for the future.

6. Parents need to be given time.

The loss of a baby, whether through miscarriage, stillbirth or neonatal death, often happens with an intensity and speed that makes it difficult for the experience to be grasped and understood.

Parents need:

- Time with each other and/or with their family.
- Time, if wanted, with their baby.
- Time to consider and make decisions about practical arrangements.
- Time in which to relive, think and talk about what has happened.

7. All those involved in the care of bereaved parents should be well informed.

Professionals who are in close contact with bereaved parents and are responsible for their care need to be well informed.

Professionals need to know:

- Their own hospital/community policy regarding the management of miscarriage, stillbirth and neonatal death.
- About statutory procedures and practical arrangements.
- About what services and support are available to parents locally.
- About grief and grieving, particularly in relation to miscarriage, stillbirth or neonatal death.

- They need this information in order to give accurate and comprehensive information to parents, since only then can parents make informed choices.

8. All those who care for and support bereaved parents should have access to support for themselves.
Professionals whose job is to care for and support bereaved parents are likely to need support themselves.

The stress involved in the care of bereaved parents is lessened if the professionals concerned:

- Receive recognition that their work is demanding and difficult and that they therefore need support, not because of professional inadequacy or personal weakness, but as a necessity.
- Have received appropriate training.
- Are working within the framework of a clear operational policy.
- Feel confident that what they are doing or being asked to do is appropriate.
- Are able to work in co-operation with other professionals.
- Are given opportunities to explore, understand and express their own feelings – both about bereavement and grief in general and also in relation to specific cases in which they are involved.

The above summary is based on the Principles of Good Practice, which appear in SANDS' *Guidelines for Professionals: Pregnancy Loss and the Death of a Baby*, by Nancy Kohner (1995). The Guidelines are available from SANDS, 28 Portland Place, London, W1B 1LY. Tel: 020 7436 7940. Website: www.uk-sands.org. Reproduced with permission.

Web Resources

Centering Corporation (Grief Resource Centre)
http://www.centering.org/

Compassionate Friends (UK)
http://www.tcf.org.uk/

European Network of Health Care Chaplains
http://eurochaplains.org/

Hospital Chaplaincy Gateway
http://www.hospitalchaplain.com/

Gundersen Lutheran (RTS)
http://www.gundluth.org/

Hygeia – online journal for bereaved parents
http://www.hygeia.org/

ISANDS – Irish Stillbirth and Neonatal Death Society
http://www.isands.ie/

Miscarriage Association (UK)
        http://www.the-ma.org.uk/

Miscarriage Association of Ireland
        http://www.coombe.ie/mai/index.html

Pregnancy and Infant Loss (SIDS Network)
        http://sids-network.org/pil.htm

Registration of Stillbirths (Irish Government)
        http://www.groireland.ie/stillbirths.htm

Registration of Stillbirths (N. Ireland)
        http://www.belfastcity.gov.uk/bdm/howto3.htm

SANDS – Stillbirth and Neonatal Death Society
        http://www.uk-sands.org/

Selected Bibliography

Borg, S., and Kasker J., *When Pregnancy Fails, Coping with Miscarriage, Stillbirth and Infant Death* (Routledge & Keegan Paul, London, 1982).

Cecil, R., *The Anthropology of Pregnancy Loss* (Berg, Oxford, 1996).

DeFrain, D.J., *Stillborn – The Invisible Death* (D.C. Heath & Co., Lexington, 1986).

Leon, I., *When a Baby Dies – Psychotherapy for Pregnancy and Newborn Loss* (Yale University, New York, 1990).

Limbo, R., Wheeler, S., *When a Baby Dies – A Handbook for Healing and Helping* (Lutheran Hospital La Crosse, 1998).

Lovell, A., *A Bereavement With a Difference. A Study of Late Miscarriage, Stillbirth and Perinatal Death* (South Bank University, London, 1983).

Moe, T., *Pastoral Care in Pregnancy Loss – A Ministry Long Needed* (Haworth Pastoral Press, New York, 1997).

Moulder, C., *Miscarriage: Women's Experience and Needs* (Pandora Press, London, 1990).

Payne, S., Horn, S. and Relf, M., *Loss and Bereavement* (Open University Press, Buckingham, 1999).

Ramshaw, E.J., *Ritual and Pastoral Care* (Fortress Press, Philadelphia, 1987).

Rando, T., *When Someone You Love Dies* (Research Press, Champaign Ill., 1991).

Shapiro, E.R., *Grief as a Family Process – A Developmental Approach to Clinical Practice* (Guilford Press, New York, 1994).

Smith, N., *Miscarriage, Stillbirth and Neonatal Death,* The Joint Committee for Hospital Chaplaincy (Ludo Press, London, 1993).

Staudacher, C., *Men and Grief* (New Harbinger Publications, California, 1991).

Sullender, R.S., *Grief & Growth, Pastoral Responses for Emotional and Spiritual Growth* (Paulist Press, New York, 1985).

Tony, W., *Funerals and How to Improve Them* (Hodder & Stoughton, London, 1990).

Woods, J.R. and Woods, J.L., *Loss During Pregnancy or in the Newborn Period* (Janetti Publications, New Jersey, 1997).

Wretmark, A.A., *Perinatal Death as a Pastoral Problem* (Almqvist & Wiksell Int., Stockholm, 1993).

Index

A

Anglican Communion   74, 82
Attitudes
    from the past   19
    changes in   21
Attachment theory   26

B

Baptism   81
    Church law on   82
    Nature of the
    request   86

Bibliography   140

C

Caring Professions: 55
    Clergy and those
    in Pastoral Care   60
    Nursing/Midwife   59
    Medical   56
    Role of the
    Professional   65

D

Depression   41

E

Ectopic pregnancy   13, 34

F

Funerals
    Children   52

Future Developments   99

G

Grief   24
    Bittersweet   49
    Children   49
    Complicated   70
    In a family setting   28
    Shadow grief   48
    Stages of   27
    Theory of   25

H

Having another baby   44

I

Islamic Tradition   77

J
Jewish Tradition 76

L
Limbo 84

M
Memorial Services 78

Methodist Church 76, 83

Miscarriage
    Common causes 33
    Definitions 13
    Types of 13
    Statistics 15

N
Nature of Loss
    Implications for
    relationship 42
    General 36
    Father 40
    Grandparents 52
    Mother 38
    Siblings 49

Naming 89

O
Original Sin 84

P
Pregnancy
    Nature of 31
    Misunderstandings
    about Pregnancy
    Loss 32

Preparing liturgy &
    services 79

Presbyterian Church 76

Principles of Good Practice
    (SANDS) 133

R
Resources
    Funeral Service 109
    Memorial Service 112
    Meditations 127
    Occasional Prayers 116
    Resources from
    other sources 130
    Scripture Resources 125
    Services of Blessing 102, 103
    Service for all faiths 104
    Service for the Family
    in a Home Setting 106
    Web Resources 138

Ritual 73

Roman Catholic Church 75, 82

S
Stillbirth
    Common causes 35
    Definition 14
    In utero 46
    Registration 14
    Statistics 15

Support Groups 91
    Changing the Attitudes
    of the Past 94
    Compassionate
    Friends 97
    ISANDS 96
    MAI 96
    SANDS 95
    SHARE 96

Liturgy from   77
What they offer   92

T
Teenage pregnancy   47

Twin
    Death of   46

U
United Reformed Church 83

W
What can be done to help?
    In the Short Term   66
    Families and
    Friends   67
    Follow up   70
    Holding and Seeing
    the Baby   68
    Photography   69